Also by John McPhee

Draft No. 4

Draft No. 4

John McPhee

On the Writing Process

Farrar, Straus and Giroux   New York

Farrar, Straus and Giroux
18 West 18th Street, New York 10011

These essays first appeared, in slightly different form, in *The New Yorker.*

Library of Congress Cataloging-in-Publication Data
Names: McPhee, John, 1931– author.
Title: Draft no. 4 : essays about the writing process / John McPhee.
Description: First edition. | New York : Farrar, Straus and Giroux,
  2017.
Identifiers: LCCN 2016059416 | ISBN 9780374142742 (hardcover) |
  ISBN 9780374712396 (ebook)
Subjects: LCSH: Authorship. | Creation (Literary, artistic, etc.) |
  English language—Rhetoric.
Classification: LCC PN149 .M43 2017 | DDC 808.02—dc23
LC record available at https://lccn.loc.gov/2016059416

Designed by Jonathan D. Lippincott

Our books may be purchased in bulk for promotional, educational, or business
use. Please contact your local bookseller or the Macmillan Corporate
and Premium Sales Department at 1-800-221-7945, extension 5442,
or by e-mail at MacmillanSpecialMarkets@macmillan.com.

www.fsgbooks.com
www.twitter.com/fsgbooks • www.facebook.com/fsgbooks

1   3   5   7   9   10   8   6   4   2

Author's Note

This book derives from eight essays on the writing process that have appeared in *The New Yorker*. One of them— "Checkpoints"—was included in a miscellaneous collection called *Silk Parachute*, but to a far greater extent belongs here, and is republished here.

Contents

Draft No. 4

Progression

A B C
———————
D

In the late nineteen-sixties, I was working in rented space on
Nassau Street up a flight of stairs and over Nathan Kasrel,
Optometrist. Across the street was the main library of Princeton University. Across the hall was the Swedish Massage. Oper-
ated by an Austrian couple who were nearing retirement and
had been there for decades, it was a legitimate business. They
massaged everything from college football players to arthritic
ancients, and they didn't give sex. This, however, was the era
when massage became a sexual synonym, and most evenings—
avoiding writing, looking down from my window on the passing scene—I would see men in business suits stop, hesitate,
look around, and then move toward the glass door at the foot
of the stairs. Eventually, the Austrians had to scrape the words
"Swedish Massage" off the door, and replace them with a hanging sign they removed when they went home at night. Meanwhile, the men kept arriving at the top of the stairs, where
neither door was marked. When they knocked on mine and I

opened it, their faces fell dramatically as the busty Swede they expected turned into a short and bearded man.

In this context, I wrote three related pieces that became a book called *Encounters with the Archdruid*. To a bulletin board I had long since pinned a sheet of paper on which I had written, in large block letters, ABC/D. The letters represented the structure of a piece of writing, and when I put them on the wall I had no idea what the theme would be or who might be A or B or C, let alone the denominator D. They would be real people, certainly, and they would meet in real places, but everything else was initially abstract.

That is no way to start a writing project, let me tell you. You begin with a subject, gather material, and work your way to structure from there. You pile up volumes of notes and then figure out what you are going to do with them, not the other way around. In 1846, in *Graham's Magazine*, Edgar Allan Poe published an essay called "The Philosophy of Composition," in which he described the stages of thought through which he had conceived of and eventually written his poem "The Raven." The idea began in the abstract. He wanted to write something tonally sombre, sad, mournful, and saturated with melancholia, he knew not what. He thought it should be repetitive and have a one-word refrain. He asked himself which vowel would best serve the purpose. He chose the long "o." And what combining consonant, producibly doleful and lugubrious? He settled on "r." Vowel, consonant, "o," "r." Lore. Core. Door. Lenore. Quoth the Raven, "Nevermore." Actually, he said "nevermore" was the first such word that crossed his mind. How much cool truth there is in that essay is in the eye of the reader.

Nonetheless, I was doing something like it when I put ABC/D on the wall. For more than a decade, first at *Time* magazine and then at *The New Yorker*, I had been writing profiles—each, by definition, portraying an individual. At *Time*,

I did countless sketches, long and short, of show-business people (Richard Burton, Sophia Loren, Barbra Streisand, et al.), and at *The New Yorker* even longer pieces, on an athlete, a headmaster, an art historian, an expert on wild food. After ten years of that, I was a little desperate to escalate, or at least get out of a groove that might turn into a rut.

To prepare a profile of an individual, the reporting endeavor looks something like this:

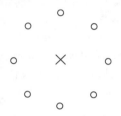

The X is the person you are principally going to talk to, spend time with, observe, and write about. The O's represent peripheral interviews with people who can shed light on the life and career of X—her friends, or his mother, old teachers, teammates, colleagues, employees, enemies, anybody at all, the more the better. Cumulatively, the O's provide triangulation— a way of checking facts one against another, and of eliminating apocrypha. Writers like Mark Singer and Brock Brower have said that you know you've done enough peripheral interviewing when you meet yourself coming the other way.

So, after those ten years and feeling squeezed in the form, I thought about doing a double profile, through a process like this:

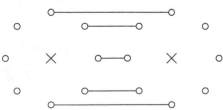

In the resonance between the two sides, added dimension might develop. Maybe I would twice meet myself coming the other way. Or four times. Who could tell what might happen? In any case, one plus one should add up to more than two.

Then who? What two people? I thought of various combinations: an actor and a director, a pitcher and a manager, a dancer and a choreographer, a celebrated architect and a highly successful bullheaded client, $1+1=2.6$. One day while I was still undecided, I happened to watch on CBS a men's semifinal in the first United States Open Tennis Championships. Two Americans—one of them twenty-five years old, the other twenty-four—were playing each other. One was white, the other black. One had grown up beside a playground in inner-city Richmond, the other on Wimbledon Road in Cleveland's wealthiest suburb. On their level are so few tennis players—and the places they compete are so organized nationally—that these two would have known each other since they were eleven years old. For something like three weeks, I kept thinking about that combination and its possibilities, and then decided to attempt a double portrait, letting the match itself contain and structure the story. I would not be able to do that without a copy of the CBS tape. In those days, tapes were not archived. They saw repeated use. The copying would have to be done as something called a kinescope—a sixteen-millimeter film shot from a television monitor. I asked William Shawn, *The New Yorker*'s editor, if he would pay for the kinescope. "Very well," he said, sighing. "Go ahead." I called CBS. A guy there said, "You haven't called a minute too soon. That tape is scheduled to be erased this afternoon."

Called "Levels of the Game," the double profile worked out, and my aspirations went into a vaulting mode. If two made sense, why not four people in one complex piece of writing? That was when I put the block letters on the bulletin board. A, B, and C would be separate from one another, and each would interact with D, yes, but who were these people? As things would eventuate, the two projects I am describing—$1+1=2.6$ and ABC/D—would be the only ones I would ever do that began as abstract expressions in search of subject matter. Quoth the raven, "Nevermore." Meanwhile, there was still no theme for the quadripartite profile. What to write about?

As I have noted in (among other places) the introduction to a book of excerpts called *Outcroppings*, a general question about any choice of subject is, Why choose that one over all other concurrent possibilities? Why does someone whose interest is to write about real people and real places choose certain people, certain places? For nonfiction projects, ideas are everywhere. They just go by in a ceaseless stream. Since you may take a month, or ten months, or several years to turn one idea into a piece of writing, what governs the choice? I once made a list of all the pieces I had written in maybe twenty or thirty years, and then put a check mark beside each one whose subject related to things I had been interested in before I went to college. I checked off more than ninety per cent.

My father was a medical doctor who dealt with the injuries of Princeton University athletes. He also travelled the world as the chief physician of several United States Olympic teams. When I was very young, he spent summers as the physician at a boys' camp in Vermont. It was called Keewaydin and was a classroom of the woods. It specialized in canoe trips and taught ecology in our modern sense when the word was still connoting the root-and-shoot relations of communal plants. Aged six to twenty, I grew up there, ending as a leader of those trips. I played basketball and tennis there, and on my high-school teams at home, with absolutely no idea that I was building the shells of future pieces of writing. I dreamed all year of the trips in the wild, not imagining, of course, that they would eventually lead to the Brooks Range, to the Yukon-Tanana suspect terrain, to the shiplike ridges of Nevada and the Laramide mountains of Wyoming, or that they would lead to the rapids of the Grand Canyon in the company of C over D.

The environmental movement was in its early stages in the nineteen-sixties, and I decided that it would be the subject of ABC/D, pitting an environmentalist against three natural enemies. Easier said than arranged. I still had no inkling who these people might be. In fact, if their names had somehow magically appeared before me I would not have recognized any of them. For help, I went to Washington, where my friend John Kauffmann, with whom I had once taught school, worked for the National Park Service as a planner. Components of the park system that have resulted from his studies are, among others, Cape Cod National Seashore and Gates of the Arctic National Park. With several of his colleagues and friends, we developed lists of possibilities, first for D. We were looking for people in the category of the late Aldo Leopold, "the father of wildlife ecology," whose *A Sand County Almanac* had sold two million copies; but he would have been too reasonable, as were other leading environmentalists of the day, with a bristly exception. David Brower, executive director of the Sierra Club, was described by Kauffmann and company as a feisty take-no-prisoners unilateral thinker with tossing white hair like a Pentateuchal prophet. He had a phone number in area code 415. I called him up. Several days later, he called back to say that he would do it. Meanwhile, A, B, and C—the three natural enemies—were easier to identify than to choose, and, seeking no input whatever from Brower, we made a list of seventeen. Several months later, it had been reduced to three, and among them was Floyd Dominy, the United States Commissioner of Reclamation. He built very big Western dams, and he was a very tough Western guy. As a young county agent in Wyoming, he had helped ranchers through drought after drought, and he deeply believed in the impoundment of water. In congressional hearings, he had fought Dave Brower over potential dam sites from Arizona to Alaska, and now and again Brower had defeated him. Dominy looked upon Brower as a "selfish preservationist." In an early interview at Dominy's office in the Department of the Interior, he said to me, "Dave Brower hates my guts. Why? Because I've *got* guts." As that conversation would play out in the eventual piece, Dominy went on to say,

"I can't talk to Brower, because he's so God-damned ridiculous. I can't even reason with the man. I once debated with him in Chicago, and he was shaking with fear. Once, after a hearing on the Hill, I accused him of garbling facts, and he said, 'Anything is fair in love and war.' For Christ's sake. After another hearing one time, I told him he didn't know what he was talking about, and said I wished I could show him. I wished he would come with me to the Grand Canyon someday, and he said, 'Well, save some of it, and maybe I will.' I had a steer out on my farm in the Shenandoah reminded me of Dave Brower. Two years running, we couldn't get him into the truck to go to market. He was an independent bastard that nobody could corral. That son of a bitch got into that truck, busted that chute, and away he went. So I just fattened him up and butchered him right there on the farm. I shot him right in the head and butchered him myself. That's the only way I could get rid of the bastard."

"Commissioner," I said, "if Dave Brower gets into a rubber raft going down the Colorado River, will you get in it, too?"

"Hell, yes," he said. "Hell, yes."

C plus D, then—that was the general idea of *Encounters with the Archdruid*. With A and B (Charles Park, a mining geologist, and Charles Fraser, a resort developer), the four

profiles in three parts worked out about as well as 1+1 had
done. So, at risk of getting into an exponential pathology, I
began to think of a sequence of six profiles in which a seventh
party would appear in a minor way in the first, appear again in
greater dimension in the second, grow further in the third,
and further in the fourth, fifth, and sixth, always in subordi-
nate ratio to the principal figure in each piece until becoming
the central figure in a seventh and final profile. However,
I backed away from this chimerical construction, just as I
once backed away from Mr. Shawn after he asked me to stop
by his office and suggested that I look into what it costs to run
hospitals in New York from the first Band-Aid to the last
bedpan. In Tina Brown's first year as editor of *The New Yorker*,
she suggested that I shelve the piece I was working on, and
write about murder in the Strait of Malacca. I demurred.
Those were the only two times in half a century that *The New
Yorker* has offered me an assignment.

Readers are not shy with suggestions, and the suggestions
are often good but also closer to the passions of the reader
than to this writer's. A sailor named Andy Chase wrote to me
from the deck of a tanker, describing the grave decline of the
U.S. Merchant Marine and detailing its present and historical
importance. Yawn. Then he said he felt sure that I couldn't
give a rat's ass for the fate of the Merchant Marine, but if I were
to come out on the ocean with merchant mariners I would
meet outspoken characters I would love to sketch. When he
was ashore, I visited him at his home, in Maine, and found
myself scribbling notes all day. Before long, he and I were visiting union halls in New York, Charleston, and Savannah,
looking for a ship. After *Looking for a Ship* was published, a
letter came from a truck driver, another complete stranger,
who owned his own chemical tanker. He said, "If you can go
out on the ocean with those people, you should come out on
the road with us." I wrote back, "Tell me what you do." On a

legal pad, while his tank was getting an interior wash, he wrote seven pages saying where he went with what. I corresponded with him for five years but didn't actually meet him until a day came when I got into his truck in Georgia. He said, right off, "Now, this may not work out. If it doesn't, I completely understand. Just tell me, and I'll drop you off at an airport anywhere on my route." I got out of his truck in Tacoma. In a lifetime of good suggestions arriving in the mail from ordinary readers, those are the only two I ever acted on.

Ideas are where you find them, and John Kauffmann, meanwhile, was feeding them to me as if he were making foie gras. John grew up in summers in northern New Hampshire in canoes, and we had so many common interests that ultimately about twenty per cent of my books would owe themselves in whole or in some part to his ideas—*Encounters with the Archdruid*, *The Survival of the Bark Canoe*, and *Coming into the Country*, among others. Even more so, however, new pieces can shoot up from other pieces, pursuing connections that run through the ground like rhizomes. Set one of these progressions in motion, and it will skein out in surprising ways, finally ending in some unexpected place.

In 1969, the year I spent with David Brower, he left his redwood house in Berkeley one day to fly upstate to Eureka and attend the dedication of Lady Bird Johnson Grove, in Redwood National Park. He took me with him. In the shadowy, columnar woods, we hiked in on a newly constructed driveway paved with redwood chips. Now and again, a slow black limousine overtook and passed us. Secret Service men in black suits walked beside the limos. At regular intervals along the way, red telephones stood up surreally above the ferns— landline desk telephones of the three-pound push-button vintage, unsheltered, each resting on a square redwood board supported by a redwood stake. While most attendees walked into the grove, the President of the United States and the

immediate-past President of the United States and a future
President of the United States and Senator George Murphy and
Billy Graham and Lady Bird and Pat and Nancy rolled through
in the limos on the chips. The ceremony took place on a redwood platform, elevating the presidents to a level unimpressive
in the landscape. California's Governor Reagan spoke pleasant
words of welcome and kept to himself his established opinion
that if you've seen one redwood you've seen them all. Richard
Nixon had much to say, much of which was lost on Lyndon
Johnson, seated nodding on the platform and before long so
sound asleep that his mouth fell open wider than a golf ball.

Afterward, at the airport in Eureka, Brower introduced
me to George Hartzog, director of the National Park Service,
who happened to be standing behind us in a long line of
people waiting for a flight to San Francisco. At the moment,
he told Brower, he was particularly interested in the Buffalo
River in Arkansas, because he wanted to get hold of it before
the Corps of Engineers did, or before developers did, or
before the state mucked it up. He wanted the Buffalo to become the nation's first National River. He said he had little
time for fishing now, except in streams near the capital, but he
thought he would try to spend a few days on the Buffalo and
look the river over. Brower had about as much interest in
fishing as he had in impounding water. I, though, surprised
myself (because I am shy to the point of dread) by blurting out
to George Hartzog, "Would you take me with you?"

He did. And he agreed to be the subject of a *New Yorker*
profile. And he brought his friend Tony Buford along on the
river. The Buffalo, alas, was swollen four feet above its normal
level, and the fishing was poor, bringing out in the two friends
a polarity of reaction. Buford was a self-educated Missouri
lawyer who had become the general counsel of Anheuser-Busch
and raised quarter horses on his farm, in the southeastern part

of the state. Hartzog, a licensed preacher who grew up in poverty in Smoaks, South Carolina, had also studied law on his own, and had passed the South Carolina bar. He and Buford had become friends when Hartzog was the chief Park Service ranger stationed in St. Louis to initiate the construction of the Gateway to the West—the Eero Saarinen arch. Hartzog, in effect, was the on-site representative of the client, and if you go there today and wish to ride to the top you will buy your ticket in the George B. Hartzog Visitor Center.

It was Hartzog who took a set of plans that had been lying dormant for fifteen years and built the great arch of St. Louis. Those who know the story of the arch say that had it not been for Hartzog there would be no arch. Hartzog the Ranger is a hero in St. Louis, but at this moment he is not a hero to Tony Buford. "God damn it, George, this river is a mess. There is no point fishing this God-damned river, George. The fishing is no good." Hartzog looks at Buford for a long moment, and the expression on his face indicates affectionate pity. He says, "Tony, fishing is always good." The essential difference between these friends is that Buford is an aggressive fisherman and Hartzog is a passive fisherman. Spread before Buford on the bow deck of his johnboat is an open, three-tiered tackle box that resembles the keyboard of a large theatre organ.

Buford filled a lot of his fishless time talking about the All-American Futurity, an annual race for two-year-old quarter horses in Ruidoso, New Mexico, toward which he aimed his efforts as a breeder. Its purse was nearly double the combined purses of the Kentucky Derby, the Preakness, and the Belmont Stakes, and was assembled in a kind of chain letter among quarter-horse breeders, involving the early registration of more than a thousand one-year-olds and incremental payments due every couple of months, like property taxes, and rising even faster. "You should come out to New Mexico and write about it," Buford said to me, and soon said it again. I didn't know a horse from a zebra, but before long he said it again, and—in campsites as on the river—again. "You should come out to New Mexico and write about the All-American."

None of Buford's horses showed adequate promise for the next All-American, and he scratched out and stayed home while I went to Ruidoso with my wife, Yolanda Whitman. She had grown up on horses in Connecticut, and pretty much knew what was going on when we went to the barns each day for two weeks, arriving sometimes before dawn. Quickly, we gravitated to Bill H. Smith, of Pea Ridge, Arkansas, who was there to take on the super-rich "Texas-buckled sons of bitches" from Oklahoma, California, and the aforementioned state. Those words did not belong to Bill H. Smith but to Dean Turpitt, the official starter, who played himself in the movie. His role in real life was huge. Quarter horses are much faster than Thoroughbreds, and a third of a minute after he opened the gate their quarter-mile races were over. A quarter horse had been clocked at fifty-five miles an hour, the world record for racehorses of any kind. From trial heats a week before-hand, in which every horse was timed no matter where it finished, the ten fastest horses at Ruidoso moved on to the final. Smith had a horse named Calcutta Deck, who made it to the final. In the last days and hours before the race, I was torn by conflicting emotions. Strongly, I wanted Deck to win for Bill H. Smith. Even more strongly, I wanted Deck to lose, because in doing so he would provide a better story. As I went to the rail to watch the race, I was literally split dizzy.

•

As it happened, there was one more stop in the cul-de-sac of this Levels–Archdruid–Ruidoso progression. Now and again through the years, people had called about film rights for my nonfiction stories, typically in the dead of night when some independent producer three time zones west had just finished reading *The New Yorker.* The calls had ceased to excite. I decided early that nothing comes of them. For the producer, the next stop would be a bank or a studio and he or she was never heard from again. The closest I had come was when a producer of both movies and television series optioned *Levels of the Game.* We met in New York, and he said he was going to rent the tennis stadium at Forest Hills and fill it up with extras. He filled it up with nothing, and even failed to meet his payment for the option.

After "Ruidoso" appeared in *The New Yorker,* there was a call from the producer Ray Stark, and this time (but nevermore) something came of it. Stark's Rastar Productions actually made a movie, titled *Casey's Shadow,* that starred actors celebrated at the time, Alexis Smith and Walter Matthau. Because I imagined that the film would not resemble the piece I had written, I asked that my name not appear in the credits. When *Casey's Shadow* came to the Prince Theater on U.S. 1 outside Princeton, Yolanda and I took our kids to see it. Between us, we had eight kids, most of whom were along. I settled into my seat and watched, and settled even farther, as I generally do, and by the end of the movie I was so slumped down I was all but flat on my back. With structural fidelity, the piece was telling the story I had written, changing little: Matthau came from quarter-horse country in Louisiana instead of Arkansas. For some reason, I had in my pocket an unusual number of coins, a whole lot of coins, and in the course of the movie the coins leaked out and fell in darkness to the floor. As the movie ended and the credits began to roll, I turned my back to the screen, got down on my hands and knees, and felt

around for the coins. Suddenly, there was an outburst of ap-
plause from my children. Evidently, the credits had said "This
picture is based upon . . . 'Ruidoso' by John McPhee" while I
was on the floor groping under the seat for nickels, dimes, and
pennies.

Structure

Out the back door and under the big ash was a picnic table. At the end of summer, 1966, I lay down on it for nearly two weeks, staring up into branches and leaves, fighting fear and panic, because I had no idea where or how to begin a piece of writing for *The New Yorker*. This was three and a half years before the progression described in the previous chapter. I went inside for lunch, surely, and at night, of course, but otherwise remained, much of that time, flat on my back on the table. The subject was the Pine Barrens of southern New Jersey. I had spent about eight months driving down from Princeton day after day, or taking a sleeping bag and a small tent. I had done all the research I was going to do—had interviewed woodlanders, fire watchers, forest rangers, botanists, cranberry growers, blueberry pickers, keepers of a general store. I had read all the books I was going to read, and scientific papers, and a doctoral dissertation. I had assembled enough material to fill a silo, and now I had no idea what to do with it. The piece would ultimately consist of some five thousand sentences, but for those two weeks I couldn't write even one. If I was blocked by fear, I was also stymied by inexperience. I had never tried to put so many different components—characters, description, dialogue, narrative, set pieces, humor, history, science, and so forth—into a single package.

It reminded me of Mort Sahl, the political comedian, about whom, six years earlier, I had written my first cover story at *Time* magazine. The scale was different. It was meant to be only five thousand words and a straightforward biographical sketch, appearing during the Kennedy-Nixon presidential campaigns, but the five thousand words seemed formidable to me then. With only a few days to listen to recordings, make notes, digest files from *Time* correspondents, read morgue clippings, and skim through several books, I was soon sprawled on the floor at home, surrounded by drifts of undifferentiated paper, and near tears in a catatonic swivet. As hour followed hour toward an absolute writing deadline (a condition I've never had to deal with at *The New Yorker*), I was able to produce only one sentence: "The citizen has certain misgivings." So did this citizen, and from all the material piled around me I could not imagine what scribbled note to take up next or—if I figured that out—where in the mess the note might be.

In my first three years at Princeton High School, in the late nineteen-forties, my English teacher was Olive McKee, whose self-chosen ratio of writing assignments to reading assignments seems extraordinary in retrospect and certainly differed from the syllabus of the guy who taught us in senior year. Mrs. McKee made us do three pieces of writing a week. Not every single week. Some weeks had Thanksgiving in them. But we wrote three pieces a week most weeks for three years. We could write anything we wanted to, but each composition had to be accompanied by a structural outline, which she told us to do first. It could be anything from Roman numerals I, II, III to a looping doodle with guiding arrows and stick figures. The idea was to build some form of blueprint before working it out in sentences and paragraphs. Mrs. McKee liked theatrics (she was also the school's drama coach), and she had us read our pieces in class to the other kids. She made no attempt to stop anybody from booing, hissing, or wadding paper and throwing it at the reader, all of which the kids did. In this crucible, I learned to duck while reading. I loved Mrs. McKee, and I loved that class. So—a dozen years later, when Mort Sahl was overwhelming me, and I was wallowing in all those notes and files—I thought of her and the structure sheets, and despite the approaching deadline I spent half the night slowly sorting, making little stacks of thematically or chronologically associated notes, and arranging them in an order that seemed to hang well from that lead sentence: "The citizen has certain misgivings." Then, as I do now, I settled on an ending before going back to the beginning. In this instance, I let the comedian himself have the last word: "'My considered opinion of Nixon versus Kennedy is that neither can win.'"

The picnic-table crisis came along toward the end of my second year as a *New Yorker* staff writer (a euphemistic term that means unsalaried freelance close to the magazine). In some twenty months, I had submitted half a dozen pieces, short and long, and the editor, William Shawn, had bought them all. You would think that by then I would have developed some confidence in writing a new story, but I hadn't, and never would. To lack confidence at the outset seems rational to me. It doesn't matter that something you've done before worked out well. Your last piece is never going to write your next one for you. Square 1 does not become Square 2, just Square 1 squared and cubed. At last it occurred to me that Fred Brown, a seventy-nine-year-old Pine Barrens native, who lived in a shanty in the heart of the forest, had had some connection or other to at least three-quarters of those Pine Barrens topics whose miscellaneity was giving me writer's block. I could introduce him as I first encountered him when I crossed his floorless vestibule—"Come in. Come in. Come on the hell in"—and then describe our many wanderings around the woods together, each theme coming up as something touched upon it. After what turned out to be about thirty thousand words, the rest could take care of itself. Obvious as it had not seemed, this organizing principle gave me a sense of a nearly complete structure, and I got off the table.

Structure has preoccupied me in every project I have undertaken since, and, like Mrs. McKee, I have hammered it at Princeton writing students across decades of teaching: "You can build a strong, sound, and artful structure. You can build a structure in such a way that it causes people to want to keep turning pages. A compelling structure in nonfiction can have an attracting effect analogous to a story line in fiction." Et cetera. Et cetera. And so forth, and so on.

The approach to structure in factual writing is like returning from a grocery store with materials you intend to cook for dinner. You set them out on the kitchen counter, and what's there is what you deal with, and all you deal with. If something is red and globular, you don't call it a tomato if it's a bell pepper. To some extent, the structure of a composition dictates itself, and to some extent it does not. Where you have a free hand, you can make interesting choices—for example, when I was confronted with the even more complicated set of notes resulting from twelve months of varied travels with the four principal participants in *Encounters with the Archdruid*. The simplified, conceptual structure ABC/D now needed filling in. There would be three sections narrating three journeys: A, in the North Cascades with Charles Park, the mining geologist; B, on a Georgia island with Charles Fraser, the resort developer; C, on the Colorado River in the Grand Canyon with Floyd Dominy, builder of huge dams. D—David Brower, the high priest of the Sierra Club—would be in all three parts. Biographical descriptions of the others would of course belong in the relevant sections, but in the stories of the three journeys the details of Brower's life could go anywhere. When I was through studying, separating, defining, and coding the whole body of notes, I had thirty-six three-by-five cards, each with two or three code words representing a component of the story. All I had to do was put them in order. What order? An essential part of my office furniture in those years was a standard sheet of plywood—four by eight feet—on two sawhorses. I strewed the cards face-up on the plywood. The anchored segments would be easy to arrange, but the free-floating ones would make the piece. I didn't stare at those cards for two weeks, but I kept an eye on them all afternoon. Finally, I found myself looking back and forth between two cards. One said "Alpinist." The other said "Upset Rapid." "Alpinist" could go anywhere. "Upset Rapid" had to be where it belonged in the journey on the river. I put the two cards side by side, "Upset Rapid" to the left. Gradually, the thirty-four other cards assembled around them until what had been strewn all over the plywood was now in neat rows. Nothing in that arrangement changed across the many months of writing.

The Colorado River in the Grand Canyon had several rapids defined on our river maps as "cannot be run without risk of life," Upset Rapid among them. We were in a neoprene raft with a guide named Jerry Sanderson, and by rule he had to stop and study the heavier rapids before proceeding down them. For several days, Brower and Dominy had been engaged in verbal artillery over Dominy's wish to build high dams in the middle of the Grand Canyon. They fought all day and half the night, while I scribbled notes. Now,

> We all got off the raft and walked to the edge of the rapid with Sanderson. . . . The problem was elemental. On the near right was an enormous hole, fifteen feet deep and many yards wide, into which poured a scaled-down

Canadian Niagara—tons upon tons of water per second. On the far left, just beyond the hole, a very large boulder was fixed in the white torrent. . . .

"What are you going to do about this one, Jerry?"

Sanderson spoke slowly and in a voice louder than usual, trying to pitch his words above the roar of the water. "You have to try to take ten per cent of the hole. If you take any more of the hole, you go in it, and if you take any less you hit the rock."

"What's at the bottom of the hole, Jerry?"

"A rubber raft," someone said.

Sanderson smiled.

"What happened two years ago, Jerry?"

"Well, the man went through in a neoprene pontoon boat, and it was cut in half by the rock. His life jacket got tangled in a boat line and he drowned. . . ."

We got back on the raft and moved out into the river. The raft turned slowly and began to move toward the rapid. "Hey," Dominy said. "Where's Dave? Hey! We left behind one of our party. We're separated now. Isn't he going to ride?" Brower had stayed on shore. We were now forty feet out. "Well, I swear, I swear, I swear," Dominy continued, slowly. "He isn't coming with us." The Upset Rapid drew us in.

With a deep shudder, we dropped into a percentage of the hole—God only knows if it was ten—and the raft folded almost in two.

As we emerged on the far side, Dominy was still talking about "the great outdoorsman" who was "standing safely on dry land wearing a God-damned life jacket." Abandoning my supposedly detached role in all this, I urged Dominy not to say anything when Dave, having walked around the rapid, rejoined us. Dominy said, "Christ, I wouldn't think of it. I wouldn't dream of it. What did he do during the war?" Brower was waiting for us when we touched the riverbank in quiet water.

Dominy said, "Dave, why didn't you ride through the rapid?"
Brower said, "Because I'm chicken."

That was the end of "Upset Rapid," and it was followed in the printed story by a half-inch or so of white space. After the white space, this:

A *Climber's Guide to the High Sierra* (Sierra Club, 1954) lists thirty-three peaks in the Sierra Nevada that were first ascended by David Brower. "Arrowhead. First ascent September 5, 1937, by David R. Brower and Richard M. Leonard. . . . Glacier Point. First ascent May 28, 1939, by Raffi Bedayn, David R. Brower, and Richard M. Leonard. . . ."

The new section went on to describe Brower as a rope-and-piton climber of the first order, who had clung by his fingernails to dizzying rock faces and granite crags. The white space that separated the Upset Rapid and the alpinist said things that I would much prefer to leave to the white space to say—violin phraseology about courage and lack of courage and how they can exist side by side in the human breast. In the juxtaposition of those two cards lay what made this phase of the writing process the most interesting to me, the most absorbing and exciting. Those two weeks on the picnic table notwithstanding, it has also always been the briefest. After putting the two cards together, and then constructing around them the rest of the book, all I had to do was write it, and that took more than a year.

•

Developing a structure is seldom that simple. Almost always there is considerable tension between chronology and theme, and chronology traditionally wins. The narrative wants to move from point to point through time, while topics that have arisen now and again across someone's life cry out to be collected. They want to draw themselves together in a single body, in the way that salt does underground. But chronology usually dominates. On tablets in Babylonia, most pieces were written that way, and nearly all pieces are written that way now. After ten years of it at *Time* and *The New Yorker*, I felt both rutted and frustrated by always knuckling under to the sweep of chronology, and I longed for a thematically dominated structure.

In 1967, after spending a few weeks interviewing the art historian Thomas P. F. Hoving, who had recently been made director of the Metropolitan Museum, I found in going over my notes that his birth-to-present chronology was particularly unaccommodating to various themes. For example, he knew a whole lot about art forgery. As a teen-ager in New York, he came upon "Utrillos," a "Boudin," and a "Renoir" in a shop in the East Fifties, and sensed that they were fakes. Eight or ten years later, as a graduate student, he sensed wrong and was stung in Vienna by an art dealer selling "hot" canvases from "Budapest" during the Hungarian Revolution. Actually, they were forgeries turned out the previous day in Vienna. In later and wiser years, he could not help admiring Han van Meegeren, who created an entire fake early period for Vermeer. In the same manner, he admired Alfredo Fioravanti, who fooled the world with his Etruscan warriors, which were lined up in the Met's Greek and Roman galleries until they were discovered to be forgeries. Most of all, he came to appreciate the wit of a talented crook who copied a silver censer and then put his tool marks on the original. At one point, Hoving studied the use of scientific instruments that help detect forgery. He even practiced forgery so he could learn to recognize it. All this having to do with the theme of forgery was scattered all over the chronology of his life. So what was I going to do to cover the theme of art and forgery? How was I going to handle, in this material, the many other examples of chronology versus theme? Same as always, chronology foremost? I threw up my hands and reversed direction. Specifically, I remembered a Sunday morning, when the museum was "dark" and I had walked with Hoving through its twilighted spaces, and we had lingered in a small room that contained perhaps two dozen portraits. A piece of writing about a single person could be presented as any number of discrete portraits, each distinct from the others and thematic in character, leaving the chronology of the subject's life to look after itself.

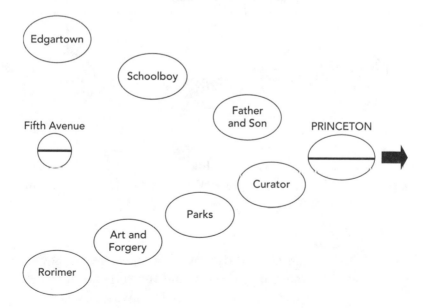

Hoving had been, to put it mildly, an unpromising youth. For example, after slugging a teacher he had been expelled from Exeter. As a freshman at Princeton, his highest accomplishment was "flagrant neglect." How did Peck's rusticated youth ever become an art historian and the director of one of the world's greatest museums? The structure's two converging arms were designed to ask and answer that question. They meet in a section that consists of just two very long paragraphs. Paragraph 1 relates to the personal arm, Paragraph 2 relates to the professional arm, and Paragraph 2 answers the question. Or was meant to.

•

Other pieces from that era were variously chronological, none more so than this one, where the clock runs left to right in both the main time line and the set pieces hanging from it:

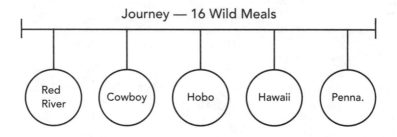

Written in 1968 and called "A Forager," it was a profile of the wild-food expert Euell Gibbons, told against the background of a canoe-and-backpacking journey on the Susquehanna River and the Appalachian Trail.

•

"Travels in Georgia" (1973) described an episodic journey of eleven hundred miles in the state, and the story would work best, I thought, if I started not on Day 1 but with a later scene involving a policeman and a snapping turtle:

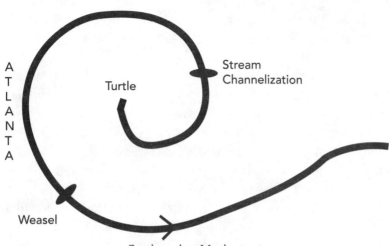

So the piece flashed back to its beginnings and then ran forward and eventually past the turtle and on through the remaining occurrences. As a nonfiction writer, you could not change the facts of the chronology, but with verb tenses and other forms of clear guidance to the reader you were free to do a flashback if you thought one made sense in presenting the story.

•

Here, in greater detail, is one more example from the nineteen-seventies, when I spent three years going back and forth to Alaska, summer and winter, on trips of as little as one month and as much as four. Three compositions resulted, each with its own structure. They were published in book form in 1977 as *Coming into the Country*. The first part—"The Encircled River"—described a canoe-and-kayak journey in Arctic Alaska, and I would like to go through its structure one component at a time. First this:

17a 18 19 20 21-13 14 15 16 17b

The numbers are calendar days. In northwest Alaska, that's how many days it takes to paddle from the Brooks Range divide to Kiana.

What impresses someone most of all about the Arctic world are its cycles. Meteorological cycles, biological cycles. Pendular swings in the populations of salmon, sheefish, caribou, lynx, snowshoe hare. Cycles unaffected by people. The wilderness operating in its own way. Seasonal cycles, annual cycles, cycles of five, ten, fifty, a hundred years. Cycles of the present and the past. This would obviously be an essential theme for a piece of writing about such terrain. We are dealing with a journey in a certain piece of time, and the piece of time can be something more than just a string of numbers. Possibly we can bend it and bring it upon itself, possibly find a structure—a structure that makes sense and is not just clever—that looks like this:

And start here, for good reason, on the fifth day of the journey, not the first.

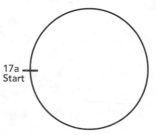

There's no throat clearing. You are right in the middle of things, and you choose the present tense for its immediacy.

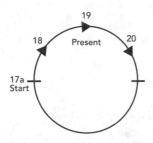

You introduce the river and the five people on it with you and the arguments and themes of the piece, while you move the boats downstream. Suddenly the trip ends. What's this? Well, the story doesn't end, because the end of the trip is followed by a flashback.

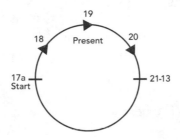

Unlike most flashbacks, however, this one is going to stay back. It will almost complete the cycle, and that moment will be the end. The piece of writing has itself been a cycle—told in the present tense and then in the past.

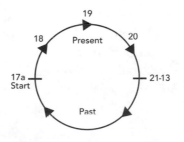

On the first day of the journey, after being helicoptered with the boats to a point near the headwaters of the river, we all went off exploring on foot. Three of us made a fourteen-mile hike around a small mountain. After ten miles or so,

We passed first through stands of fireweed, and then over ground that was wine-red with the leaves of bear-berries. There were curlewberries, too, which put a deep-purple stain on the hand. We kicked at some wolf scat, old as winter. It was woolly and white and filled with the hair of a snowshoe hare. Nearby was a rich inventory of caribou pellets and, in increasing quantity as we moved downhill, blueberries—an outspreading acreage of blueberries. Fedeler stopped walking. He touched my arm. He had in an instant become even more alert than he usually was, and obviously apprehensive. His gaze followed straight on down our intended course. What he saw there I saw now. It appeared to me to be a hill of fur. "Big boar grizzly," Fedeler said in a near-whisper. The bear was about a hundred steps away, in the blueberries, grazing. The head was down, the hump high. The immensity of muscle seemed to vibrate slowly—to expand and contract, with the grazing. Not berries alone but whole bushes were going into the bear. He was big for a barren-ground grizzly. The brown bears of Arctic Alaska (or grizzlies; they are no longer thought to be different) do not grow to the size they will reach on more ample diets elsewhere. The barren-ground grizzly will rarely grow larger than six hundred pounds. "What if he got too close?" I said. Fedeler said, "We'd be in real trouble." "You can't outrun them," Hession said. A grizzly, no slower than a racing horse, is about half again as fast as the fastest human being.

Watching the great mound of weight in the blueberries, with a fifty-five-inch waist and a neck more than thirty inches around, I had difficulty imagining that he could move with such speed, but I believed it, and was without impulse to test the proposition.

That particular encounter occurred close to the start of the nine-day river trip. That bear would be, to say the least, a difficult act to follow. One dividend of this structure is that the grizzly encounter occurs about three-fifths of the way along, a natural place for a high moment in any dramatic structure.

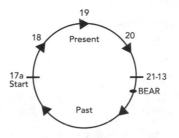

And it also occurs just where and when it happened on the trip. You're a nonfiction writer. You can't move that bear around like a king's pawn or a queen's bishop. But you can, to an important and effective extent, arrange a structure that is completely faithful to fact.

On down the river we go.

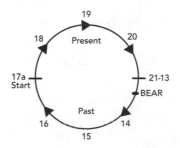

All through the composition, the text in various ways reveals its absorption with the cyclic theme. An example near the beginning:

In the sixteenth century, the streams of eastern America ran clear (except in flood), but after people began taking the vegetation off the soil mantle and then leaving their fields fallow when crops were not there, rain carried the soil into the streams. The process continues, and when one looks at such streams today, in their seasonal varieties of chocolate, their distant past is—even to the imagination—completely lost. For this Alaskan river, on the other hand, the sixteenth century has not yet ended, nor the fifteenth, nor the fifth. The river flows, as it has since immemorial time, in balance with itself. The river and every rill that feeds it are in an unmodified natural state—opaque in flood, ordinarily clear, with levels that change within a closed cycle of the year and of the years. The river cycle is only one of many hundreds of cycles—biological, meteorological— that coincide and blend here in the absence of intruding artifice. Past to present, present reflecting past, the cycles compose this segment of the earth. It is not static, so it cannot be styled "pristine," except in the special sense that while human beings have hunted, fished, and gathered wild food in this valley in small groups for centuries, they have not yet begun to change it.

And another, toward the end:

What had struck me most in the isolation of this wilderness was an abiding sense of paradox. In its raw, convincing emphasis on the irrelevance of the visitor, it was forcefully, importantly repellent. It was no less strongly attractive—with a beauty of nowhere else, composed in turning circles. If the wild land was indifferent, it gave a sense of difference. If at moments it was frightening, requiring an effort to put down the conflagrationary imagination, it also augmented the touch of life. This was not a dare with nature. This was nature.

And finally, at the end, just before the loop would close, we come upon another bear.

He was young, possibly four years old, and not much over four hundred pounds. He crossed the river. He studied the salmon in the riffle. He did not see, hear, or smell us. Our three boats were close together, and down the light current on the flat water we drifted toward the fishing bear.

He picked up a salmon, roughly ten pounds of fish, and, holding it with one paw, he began to whirl it around his head. Apparently, he was not hungry, and this was a form of play. He played sling-the-salmon. With his claws embedded near the tail, he whirled the salmon and then tossed it high, end over end. As it fell, he scooped it up and slung it around his head again, lariat salmon, and again he tossed it into the air. He caught it and heaved it high once more. The fish flopped to the ground. The bear turned away, bored. He began to move upstream by the edge of the river. Behind his big head his hump projected. His brown fur rippled like a field under wind. He kept coming. The breeze was behind him. He had not yet seen us. He was romping along at an easy walk. As he came closer to us, we drifted slowly toward him. The single Klepper, with John Kauffmann in it, moved up against a snagged stick and broke it off. The snap was light, but enough to stop the bear. Instantly, he was motionless and alert, remaining on his four feet and straining his eyes to see. We drifted on toward him. At last, we arrived in his focus. If we were looking at something we had rarely seen before, God help him so was he.

He seems to fit at the end, to provide a final scene, and the structure makes it work that way—although the encounter occurred in the exact middle of the trip.

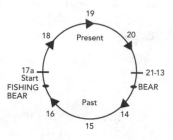

Readers are not supposed to notice the structure. It is meant to be about as visible as someone's bones. And I hope this structure illustrates what I take to be a basic criterion for all structures: they should not be imposed upon the material. They should arise from within it. That perfect circle was a help to me, but it could be a liability for anyone trying to impose such a thing on just any set of facts. A structure is not a cookie cutter. Certain Baroque poets, among others, wrote shaped verse, in which lines were composed so that the typography resembled the topic—blossoms, birds, butterflies. That also is not what I mean by structure. A piece of writing has to start somewhere, go somewhere, and sit down when it gets there. You do that by building what you hope is an unarguable structure. Beginning, middle, end. Aristotle, Page 1.

•

Each of those structures, from the nineteen-sixties and nineteen-seventies, was worked out after copying with a typewriter all notes from notebooks and transcribing the contents of microcassettes. I used an Underwood 5, which had once been a state-of-the-art office typewriter but by 1970 had been outclassed by the I.B.M. Selectric. With the cassettes, I used a Sanyo TRC5200 Memo-Scriber, which was activated with foot pedals, like a sewing machine or a pump organ. The note-typing could take many weeks, but it collected everything in one legible place, and it ran all the raw material in some concentration through the mind.

The notes from one to the next frequently had little in common. They jumped from topic to topic, and only in places were sequentially narrative. So I always rolled the platen and left blank space after each item to accommodate the scissors that were fundamental to my advanced methodology. After reading and rereading the typed notes and then developing the structure and then coding the notes accordingly in the margins and then photocopying the whole of it, I would go at the copied set with the scissors, cutting each sheet into slivers of varying size. If the structure had, say, thirty parts, the slivers would end up in thirty piles that would be put into thirty manila folders. One after another, in the course of writing, I would spill out the sets of slivers, arrange them ladderlike on a card table, and refer to them as I manipulated the Underwood. If this sounds mechanical, its effect was absolutely the reverse. If the contents of the seventh folder were before me, the contents of twenty-nine other folders were out of sight. Every organizational aspect was behind me. The procedure eliminated nearly all distraction and concentrated just the material I had to deal with in a given day or week. It painted me into a corner, yes, but in doing so it freed me to write.

Cumbersome aspects there may have been, but the scissors, the slivers, the manila folders, the three-by-five cards, and the Underwood 5 were my principal tools until 1984, a year in which I was writing about a schoolteacher in Wyoming and quoting frequently from a journal she began in 1905. Into several late drafts of that piece, I laboriously typed and re-typed those journal entries—another adventure in tedium. Two friends in Princeton—Will Howarth, a professor of English, and Richard Preston, one of his newly minted Ph.D.s—had been waxing evangelical for months on end about their magical computers, which were then pretty much a novelty. Preston put me in touch with Howard J. Strauss, in Princeton's Office of Information Technology. Howard had worked for NASA in Houston on the Apollo program and was now in Princeton guiding the innumerate. For a couple of decades, his contribution to my use of the computer in teaching, researching, and writing would be so extensive that—as I once wrote—if he were ever to leave Princeton I would pack up and follow him, even to Australia. When I met him in 1984, the first thing he said to me was "Tell me what you do."

He listened to the whole process from pocket notebooks to coded slices of paper, then mentioned a text editor called Kedit, citing its exceptional capabilities in sorting. Kedit (pronounced "kay-edit"), a product of the Mansfield Software Group, is the only text editor I have ever used. I have never used a word processor. Kedit did not paginate, italicize, approve of spelling, or screw around with headers, wysiwygs, thesauruses, dictionaries, footnotes, or Sanskrit fonts. Instead, Howard wrote programs to run with Kedit in imitation of the way I had gone about things for two and a half decades.

He wrote Structur. He wrote Alpha. He wrote mini-macros galore. Structur lacked an "e" because in those days in the Kedit directory eight letters was the maximum he could use in naming a file. In one form or another, some of these things have come along since, but this was 1984 and the future stopped there. Howard, who died in 2005, was the polar opposite of Bill Gates—in outlook as well as income. Howard thought the computer should be adapted to the individual and not the other way around. One size fits one. The programs he wrote for me were molded like clay to my requirements—an appealing approach to anything called an editor.

Structur exploded my notes. It read the codes by which each note was given a destination or destinations (including the dustbin). It created and named as many new Kedit files as there were codes, and, of course, it preserved intact the original set. In my first I.B.M. computer, Structur took about four minutes to sift and separate fifty thousand words. My first computer cost five thousand dollars. I called it a five-thousand-dollar pair of scissors.

I wrote my way sequentially from Kedit file to Kedit file from the beginning to the end of the piece. Some of those files created by Structur could be quite long. So each one in turn needed sorting on its own, and sometimes fell into largish parts that needed even more sorting. In such phases, Structur would have been counterproductive. It would have multiplied the number of named files, choked the directory, and sent the writer back to the picnic table, and perhaps under it. So Howard wrote Alpha. Alpha implodes the notes it works on. It doesn't create anything new. It reads codes and then churns a file internally, organizing it in segments in the order in which they are meant to contribute to the writing.

Alpha is the principal, workhorse program I run with Kedit. Used again and again on an ever-concentrating quantity of notes, it works like nesting utensils. It sorts the whole business at the outset, and then, as I go along, it sorts chapter material and subchapter material, and it not infrequently arranges the components of a single paragraph. It has completely served many pieces on its own. When I run it now, the action is instantaneous in a way that I—born in 1931—find breathtaking. It's like a light switch. I click on "Run Alpha," and in zero seconds a window appears that says, for example,

> Alpha has completed 14 codes and 1301 paragraph segments were processed. 7246 lines were read and 7914 lines were written to the sorted file.

One line is 11.7 words.

Kedit's All command helps me find all the times I use any word or phrase in a given piece, and tells me how many lines separate each use from the next. It's sort of like a leaf blower. Mercilessly, it will go after fad words like "hone," "pivot," "proactive," "icon," "iconic," "issues," "awesome," "aura," "arguably," and expressions like "reach out," "went viral," and "take it to the next level." It suggests how much of "but" is too much "but." But its principal targets are the legions of perfectly acceptable words that should not appear more than once in a piece of writing— "legions," in the numerical sense, among them, and words like "expunges," "circumvallate," "horripilation," "disjunct," "defunct," "amalgamate," "ameliorate," "defecate," and a few thousand others. Of those that show up more than once, All expunges all.

When Keditw came along—Kedit for Windows—Howard rewrote everything, and the task was not a short one. In 2007, two years after he died, a long e-mail appeared in my in-box addressed to everyone on the "KEDIT for Windows Announcement list"—Subject: "News About Kedit." It included this paragraph:

> The last major release of KEDIT, KEDIT for Windows 1.5, came out in 1996, and we are no longer actively

working on major "new feature" releases of the program. Sales have gradually slowed down over the years, and it now makes sense to gradually wind down.

It was signed "Mansfield Software Group, Storrs CT."

This is when I began to get a true sense of the tensile strength and long dimension of the limb I was out on. I replied on the same day, asking the company how much time—after half a million words in twenty-three years—I could hope to continue using Kedit. In the back-and-forth that followed, there was much useful information, and this concluding remark:

If you run into any problems with KEDIT or with those macros in the future, let me know. You will definitely get my personal attention, if only because I'll be the only one left at my company!

It was signed "Kevin Kearney."

Driving to Boston one time, I stopped in at Storrs, home of the University of Connecticut, to meet him and show him some of the things Howard Strauss had done. In this Xanadu of basketball, I found Kearney and his wife, Sara, close to the campus in a totally kempt small red house previously occupied by a UConn basketball coach. From my perspective, they looked young enough and trim enough to be shooting hoops themselves, and that to me was especially reassuring. He was wearing running shoes, a Metropolitan Museum T-shirt. He had an alert look and manner; short, graying dark hair; a clear gaze, no hint of guile—an appealing, trusting guy.

Before long, Sara went off to an appointment, leaving us at the dining table with our laptops open like steamed clams. I was awestruck to learn that he had bought his first personal computer only two years before I had, and I was bemused to contemplate the utterly disparate vectors that had carried us to the point of sale—me out of a dark cave of pure ignorance and Kearney off a mainframe computer.

He grew up in New Haven and in nearby Madison, he told me, and at UConn majored in math, but he developed an even greater interest in computer science. In those pre-PC days, people shared time on the university's mainframe—a system that was, in its way, ancestral cloud computing. Per student computer terminal, the university paid a hundred and fifty dollars a month, all caps. If the university wanted a terminal to do lowercase as well, the cost was thirty dollars higher. There were a lot of people then who thought computers were too expensive to do word processing.

The first UConn thesis ever written on a computer was done on the mainframe by a pharmacy major in 1976, when Kearney was a year past his own graduation and working in the university's computer center (where he met Sara, from Maryland, an alumna of American University, and also a computer programmer). He still did not own a personal computer and could not afford a five-thousand-dollar pair of anything. Apple II had been on the market since 1977 but did not interest him. It was "too much of a toy"—its display was only forty characters wide. The displays on I.B.M. PCs were eighty characters wide. His father helped him buy one. Five thousand dollars in 1982 translates to nearly thirteen thousand dollars at this writing.

On the mainframe, everyone from undergraduates to programmers used an evolving variety of text editors, most notably Xedit, which was written at I.B.M. by Xavier de Lamberterie and made available in 1980. Kevin Kearney was so interested in Xedit that he bought forty manuals out of his own pocket and offered them to students and faculty. Then, after the new I.B.M. PCs appeared, and he had bought his first one, an idea he addressed was how to achieve mainframe power in a PC editor. "Xedit was in a different language that only worked on mainframes," he told me. "Xedit was in mainframe assembler language, almost like machine language." What was needed was a text editor that mainframe programmers could use on their PCs at home. As companies bought PCs for their employees—as insurance programmers, for example, went home to PCs at night—the need increased. So Kearney, aged twenty-eight, cloned Xedit to accomplish that purpose. Moreover, he said, "you could do some nifty additional things that didn't exist on the mainframe. On the mainframe you couldn't scroll. You couldn't word-wrap to a new line."

Writing the initial version of Kedit took him about four months, in late 1982. Like a newborn bear cub, it amounted to the first one per cent of what it would eventually become. "There are two kinds of editors," Kearney continued. "One sees things as characters; Kedit sees it as a bunch of lines. It's more primitive, in a sense, like keypunches. Each line is like one card." He said he started with "some things from Xedit plus suggestions from others," and his goal was "convenient text editing." After a pause, he added, "I'd rather have Kedit be a good text editor than a bad word processor." He asked me to take care not to create an impression that he invented much of anything. "What I did was package in a useful way a number of ideas. I.B.M. seemed happy enough with the cloning. There was no hint that they objected."

Not remotely in the way, certainly, that Steve Jobs would object, in 1983, to what he characterized as Bill Gates's theft of Apple's mouse-driven Graphical User Interface. In an interface-to-interface encounter—described by Andy Hertzfeld, a Macintosh system designer who was present—Jobs shouted at Gates:

"You're ripping us off! I trusted you, and now you're stealing from us!" But Bill Gates just stood there coolly,

looking Steve directly in the eye, before starting to
speak in his squeaky voice. "Well, Steve, I think there's
more than one way of looking at it. I think it's more like
we both had this rich neighbor named Xerox and I
broke into his house to steal the TV set and found out
that you had already stolen it."

Kevin Kearney—who, like Jobs and Gates and the prevail-
ing demography of the digital world, was still under thirty—
began putting Kedit ads in computer magazines, where ads
were not expensive. Orders came in. "Mansfield Software
Group" was headquartered in his apartment. He went to the
campus bookstore, bought three-ring binders, and photocopied his instructions, thus making the original Kedit manual, which he sent to his customers with Kedit diskettes. At a
conference in Boston in March, 1984, Kevin and Sara met
Howard Strauss. Showing him Kedit, they were quickly taken
aback. Howard waxed animatedly critical. Still set in his own
mainframe mentality, he said, for example, "There's no prefix
area!" The prefix I.B.M. programmers were used to consisted
of five equal-signs at the beginning of each line (=====). For
technical reasons, they were useful in editing commands on
mainframe terminals. But Kevin and Sara talked with Howard about much more, and he offered useful suggestions. A
month or so later, Strauss telephoned Kearney for more talk,
and the upshot was that Princeton bought Kedit's first site
license.

At the time, the Mansfield Software Group had a roster of
one—one full-time entrepreneur. In the following year, the
company moved into office space above a liquor store that was
a kind of inholding on the UConn campus. For a decade or so
across the late eighties and early nineties, it flourished, and
the number of employees increased to as many as twelve. In

1987, a letter arrived from Barbara Tolejano, of Morgan Products Ltd., in Oshkosh, Wisconsin, who said that she had received in the mail her Kedit diskettes and manual, and had thrown "box, packing material, binder into outdoor trash container" because of "overwhelming garlic odor." Mansfield's expanding personnel liked garlicky sandwiches. The diskettes stank, too.

A version of Kedit called Kedit/Semitic was developed at Princeton in the nineteen-eighties. Its cursor popped up at the far right, and it wrote its way leftward in Hebrew and Arabic. I asked Kevin Kearney how many users, nationally and globally, Kedit has now. "Fewer than there used to be" is as close as he would come to telling me, but he said he still gets about ten e-mails a week asking for support.

"Are they essentially all from programmers, or are there other users in the e-gnorant zone like me?"

"Yes."

Kedit did not catch on in a large way at Princeton. I used to know other Kedit users—a historian of science, a Jefferson scholar. Aware of this common software, we nodded conspiratorially. Today on the campus, the number of people using Kedit is roughly one. Not long ago, I asked Jay Barnes, an information technologist at Princeton, if he thought I was enfolded in a digital time warp. "Right; yes," he said. "But you found it and it works, and you haven't switched it because of fashion." Or, as Tracy Kidder wrote in 1981, in *The Soul of a New Machine*, "Software that works is precious. Users don't idly discard it."

Kevin Kearney, who says he is "semi-retired," hopes not "to see a bunch of orders showing up," and he asked me to make clear that Kedit was "very much a thing of its time," and its time is not today. I guess I'm living evidence of that.

•

When I would thank Howard Strauss for the programs he wrote and amplified and updated, he always said, "Oh, it was no trouble; there was nothing to it; it was all simple."

For many years in my writing class, I drew structures on a blackboard with chalk. In the late nineteen-nineties, I fell off my bicycle, massively tore a rotator cuff, underwent surgery, spent months in physical therapy, and had to give up the chalk for alternative technologies. I was sixty-eight. Briefly, I worked things out with acetates and overhead projection. Enduringly, I was once again helped beyond measure by Howard Strauss.

With PowerPoint, he modernized my drawings of the structures of pieces written before I bought my first computer; and in 2005, during the last months of his life, he was still taking my rough sketches and turning them into structural presentations, some of them complicated and assisted by the use of color. Students in class would say things like "Wow, those PowerPoints are really good. How did you do that?" To which I responded, as I still do, "Oh, it was no trouble; there was nothing to it; it was all simple; Howard Strauss did it."

Showing in class the structural diagrams of "The Encircled River," I used to recite, more or less, "It's the story of a journey, and hence it represents a form of chronological structure, following that journey as it was made through space and time. There are structural alternatives, but for the story of a journey they can be unpromising and confusing when compared with a structure that is chronologically controlled." Et cetera, et cetera, in an annual mantra about what I thought to be axiomatic: journeys demand chronological structures. That was before 2002, when I went from a truck stop in Georgia to a product delivery elsewhere in Georgia to an interior wash in South Carolina to a hazmat manufacturer in North Carolina and then across the country to the State of Washington in the sixty-five-foot chemical tanker owned and driven by a guy named Don Ainsworth.

Think about it. Think how it appeared to the writer when it was still a mass of notes. The story goes from the East Coast to the West Coast of the United States. Has any other writer ever done that? Has any other writer ever not done that? Even I had done something like it in discussing North American geology in *Annals of the Former World*. You don't need to remember much past Meriwether Lewis, George R. Stewart, John Steinbeck, Bernard DeVoto, Wallace Stegner, and William Least Heat-Moon in order to discern a beaten path. If you are starting a westbound piece in, say, Savannah, can you get past Biloxi without caffeinating the prose? If Baltimore—who is going to care if you get through Cumberland Gap? New York? The Hackensack River. If you start in Boston, turn around. In a structural sense, I turned around—once again reversing a prejudice. In telling this story, the chronology of the trip would not only be awkward but would also be a liability.

Ainsworth and I started in Bankhead, Georgia, where I met him, after our five years of correspondence. When I got out of his truck in Tacoma, I had ridden three thousand one hundred and ninety miles with him.

Just the fact of those three thousand one hundred and ninety miles, if mentioned in the past tense early in the piece, might open the way to a thematic structure. The lead should be somewhere on the road in the West. The reader would see the span of the journey, the general itinerary. Thematic details could coalesce in varying categories and from all over the map in the form of set pieces on truck stops, fuel economy, driver demographics, Ainsworth's idiosyncrasies, and other topics. Where to start?

In the State of Wyoming are four thousand square miles called the Great Divide Basin, where the Continental Divide itself divides, like separating strands of old rope, surrounding a vast landscape that does not drain to the Atlantic or the Pacific. We went right through it in the chemical tanker, and I thought it might be an oddly interesting place in which to begin.

Great Divide Basin

The lead would be chronological (rolling westward), and after the random collection of themes the final segment would pick up where the first one left off and roll on through the last miles to the destination. Thus two chronological drawstrings—one at the beginning of the piece, the other at the end—would pull tight the sackful of themes.

Good idea, but I scrapped the Great Divide Basin. It was too far east. There was too much stuff from Idaho, Oregon, and so forth that ought best to be in the thematic groupings.

So, to tell of this trip from coast to coast—after establishing my own credentials with a personal preamble in the New Jersey bad-driver clinic—I started in eastern Oregon with Deadman Pass and Cabbage Hill and Ainsworth saluting a girl in a bikini.

From Atlanta and Charlotte to North Powder, Oregon, this was the first time that Ainsworth had so much as tapped his air horn. In the three thousand one hundred and ninety miles I rode with him he used it four times.

Of the seven thematic sections that followed, each, in concept, would be much like the section I coded TSG.

TSG

If there is one indispensable theme about the big behemoth trucks, it is the nature and description of truck stops generally. The principal truck stops described in the piece (and dotted here) would be in places like Kingdom City, Missouri; Bankhead, Georgia; Oak Grove, Kentucky; and Little America, Wyoming.

Explosives are carried in liquid form in tankers. The more prudent truck stops have designated "safe havens"— Class 1 parking spaces situated, if not in the next county, at least, as Ainsworth put it, "a little away from the rest of the folks who may not want to be there when the thing lights off."

. . .

I think it can be said, generally, that truckers are big, amiable, soft-spoken, obese guys. The bellies they carry are in the conversation with hot-air balloons. There are drivers who keep bicycles on their trucks, but they are about as common as owner-operators of stainless-steel chemical tankers.

In recapitulation, the structure of the story was this:

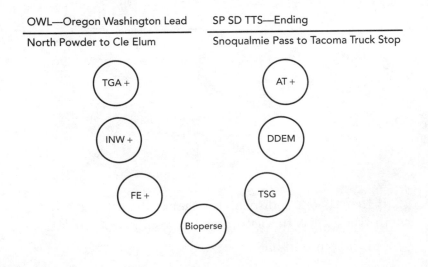

OWL—Oregon Washington Lead	SP SD TTS—Ending
North Powder to Cle Elum	Snoqualmie Pass to Tacoma Truck Stop

TGA +

AT +

INW +

DDEM

FE +

TSG

Bioperse

•

Often, after you have reviewed your notes many times and thought through your material, it is difficult to frame much of a structure until you write a lead. You wade around in your notes, getting nowhere. You don't see a pattern. You don't know what to do. So stop everything. Stop looking at the notes. Hunt through your mind for a good beginning. Then write it. Write a lead. If the whole piece is not to be a long one, you may plunge right on and out the other side and have a finished draft before you know it; but if the piece is to have some combination of substance, complexity, and structural juxtaposition that pays dividends, you might begin with that acceptable and workable lead and then be able to sit back with the lead in hand and think about where you are going and how you plan to get there. Writing a successful lead, in other words, can illuminate the structure problem for you and cause you to see the piece whole—to see it conceptually, in various parts, to which you then assign your materials. You find your lead, you build your structure, you are now free to write.

Some of these thoughts on leads, taken from my seminar notes, were printed several years ago in the Word Craft column of *The Wall Street Journal*. In slightly altered form, I'm including them here. I would go so far as to suggest that you should always write your lead (redoing it and polishing it until you are satisfied that it will serve) before you go at the big pile of raw material and sort it into a structure.

O.K. then, what is a lead? For one thing, the lead is the hardest part of a story to write. And it is not impossible to write a very bad one. Here is an egregiously bad one from an article on chronic sleeplessness. It began: "Insomnia is the triumph of mind over mattress." Why is that bad? It's not bad at all if you want to be a slapstick comedian—if humor, at that stratum, is your purpose. If you are serious about the subject, you might seem to be indicating at the outset that you don't have confidence in your material so you are trying to make up for it by waxing cute.

I have often heard writers say that if you have written your lead you have in a sense written half of your story. Finding a good lead can require that much time, anyway—through trial and error. You can start almost anywhere. Several possibilities will occur to you. Which one are you going to choose? It is easier to say what not to choose. A lead should not be cheap, flashy, meretricious, blaring. After a tremendous fanfare of verbal trumpets, a mouse comes out of a hole blinking.

Blind leads—wherein you withhold the name of the person you are writing about and reveal it after a paragraph or two—range from slightly cheap to very cheap. Don't be concerned if you have written blind leads. I've written my share of blind leads, I can tell you. There's nothing inherently wrong with them. They're so obvious, though. You should ration such indulgences through time. A blind lead is like a magician pulling a rabbit out of a hat, but the ears were sticking up from the get-go. Be conscious of the risk—of what is often wrong with such things—and then go ahead and try them. In this or that piece of mine, I have felt that a blind lead was by far the best choice. But not very often.

All leads—of every variety—should be sound. They should never promise what does not follow. You read an exciting action lead about a car chase up a narrow street. Then the article turns out to be a financial analysis of debt structures in private universities. You've been had. The lead—like the title—should be a flashlight that shines down into the story. A lead is a promise. It promises that the piece of writing is going to be like this. If it is not going to be so, don't use the lead. Some leads are much longer than others. I am not talking just about first sentences. I am talking about an integral beginning that sets a scene and implies the dimensions of the story. That might be a few words, a few hundred words. And it might be two thousand words, setting the scene for a story fifty times as long. A lead is good not because it dances, fires cannons, or whistles like a train but because it is absolute to what follows.

Another way to prime the pump is to write by hand. Keep a legal pad, or something like one, and when you are stuck dead at any time—blocked to paralysis by an inability to set one word upon another—get away from the computer, lie down somewhere with pencil and pad, and think it over. This can do wonders at any point in a piece and is especially helpful when you have written nothing at all. Sooner or later something comes to you. Without getting up, you roll over and scribble on the pad. Go on scribbling as long as the words develop. Then get up and copy what you have written into your computer file.

What counts is a finished piece, and how you get there is idiosyncratic. Alternating between handwriting and computer typing almost always moves me along, but that doesn't mean it will work for you. It just might. I knew an editor who had a lot of contempt for nearly all writers and did his own writing with a quill pen. No one approaches this topic in quite the way that Anne Tyler does, just as no one without a photocopying machine could come near *Saint Maybe, The Accidental Tourist, Breathing Lessons,* or *Dinner at the Homesick Restaurant.* "I have all kinds of superstitions about writing," she told the *Authors Guild Bulletin.* "When I'm working on a book, I write five days a week, but never on weekends or any legal holidays; I use a Parker 75 fountain pen with a nib marked 62 which, to my horror, I've discovered they no longer make, and black ink and unlined white paper; and I rewrite each draft in longhand all over again even though I'll have typed the earlier drafts into the computer, because to me writing feels like a kind of handicraft. It feels as if I'm knitting a novel."

In 1987, Wendell Berry wrote an essay called "Why I Am Not Going to Buy a Computer." He explained: "As a farmer,

I do almost all of my work with horses. As a writer, I work
with a pencil or a pen and a piece of paper. . . . I would hate to
think that my work as a writer could not be done without a
direct dependence on strip-mined coal. . . . For the same reason, it matters to me that my writing is done in the daytime,
without electric light."

Teaching *Son of the Morning Star* one year, I was full of
admiration for the way Evan S. Connell would briefly mention
something, amplify it slightly fifteen pages later, and add to it
twenty pages after that, gradually teasing up enough curiosity
to call for a full-scale set piece. This especially applied to the
war chief Gall, who spoke a few arresting words in his first appearance, more words that were even more interesting in his
second cameo, and so on through a couple of hundred pages.
This is nonfiction and these were researched quotations. Your
interest in and curiosity about Chief Gall and his heroic intelligence gradually builds to a point where you are ready to
choke the author for not telling you more. At that point,
Evan S. Connell rolls out a fine and detailed biographical portrait of the great Hunkpapa Lakota.

I wanted to cite in class each mention of Gall from Page 1
to the portrait. *Son of the Morning Star* has a very brief, very
bad index. So I wrote to Evan Connell, whom I had never
met, asking him to save me lots of time and do me the great
favor of searching the text in his computer for all mentions of
Gall, a task that surely would not take more than a few moments. Computer? he wrote back. Computer? His technology
had not risen past his portable Olivetti.

That was at the end of the twentieth century. In 2011, Lilith
Wood, a former student of mine, wrote to tell me that she was
writing a book about her native Alaska and had challenged her
computer with a typewriter—"a 1970-something Remington
Premier, bought online from a shop in Portland called Blue

Moon Camera and Machine." She went on to say, "The process was very personalized, and included phone conversations with the shop's owner. On the Web site they asked 'Are you ready to have a lasting relationship with a machine?' I really enjoy that there's no on/off switch. Oh, and it has just been so pleasurable to type on it. I put on music and really get going. I use it at a standing desk, and I really have to punch those keys."

•

In 2003, I was hoping to find a way to ride on a river towboat as part of a series of pieces on freight transportation. I had reason not to be optimistic. Corporations prepare for journalists with bug spray. They are generally less approachable than, say, the F.B.I., and, if at all agreeable, take even more precautions. I had been rebuffed flatly by various companies and jilted by some that at first said yes. Vice-presidents said yes. CEOs heard about it and said no.

Vice-president: But Adolf, this guy is fangless. He's not Seymour Hersh. He's not Upton Sinclair.

Adolf: I don't care who he is. He's a journalist, and no matter what they write no journalist is ever going to do our company any kind of good.

Against that background, and some days after writing a letter of request, I called Memco Barge Line, in St. Louis, and asked for Don Huffman. He said, "What day would you like to go?"

It was as if I were talking to Southwest Airlines. Tows are moving about the country all the time. When and where would I like to get on one? I flew to St. Louis, and went up to Grafton, where the Billy Joe Boling came along after a while and picked me off the riverbank with a powered skiff.

The river was the Illinois—barge route from the Mississippi to the outskirts of Chicago. At Grafton, in southern Illinois, the Billy Joe Boling collected its fifteen barges from larger tows in the Mississippi, wired them taut as an integral vessel, and went up the Illinois until constricting dimensions of the river forced another exchange, with a smaller towboat, and the Billy Joe Boling took a new rig of fifteen barges downstream. This endless yo-yo was not exactly a journey in the Amundsen sense. There was no vestige of a beginning, no prospect of an end. If ever there was a journey piece in which a chronological structure was pointless, this was it. In fact, a chronological structure would be misleading. Things happened, that's all—anywhere and everywhere. And they happened in themes, each of which could have its own title at the head of a section, chronology ignored.

The over-all title was "Tight-Assed River." There were eight sections. One section's title was "Calling Traffic."

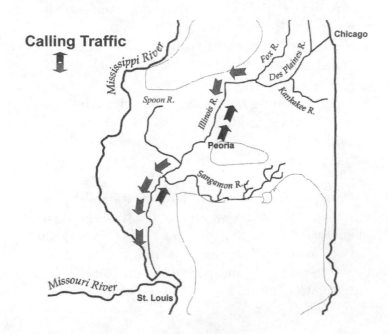

The arrows coincide with places where things happened, such as Creve Coeur Landing, Kickapoo Bend. But they are not consecutive in the story.

When I told my friend Andy Chase that I was coming out here, he said, "The way they handle those boats—gad! They go outrageous places with them. The ship handling is phenomenal." The fact notwithstanding that Andy is a licensed master of ships of any gross tons upon oceans, he said he would envy me being here. This tow is not altogether like an oceangoing ship. We are a lot longer than the Titanic, yes, but we are a good deal lighter. We weigh only thirty thousand tons. Yet that is surely enough to make our slow motion massive, momentous, tectonic. Fighting the current with full left rudder and full left flanking rudder in the eighty-degree turn at Creve Coeur Landing, Kickapoo Bend, Tom Armstrong says, "I'm trying to get it pointed up before it puts me on the bank. There's no room for maneuvering. You can't win for losing. You just don't turn that fast. You just don't stop that fast. Sometimes we don't make our turns. We have to back up. The Illinois River's such a tight-assed river."

. . .

Trains run under centralized systems. These people are self-organized, talking back and forth on VHF, planning hold-ups and advances, and signing off with the names of their vessels: "Billy Joe Boling southbound, heading into Anderson Lake country. Billy Joe Boling, southbound."

This is known as "calling traffic."

. . .

Tom calls to another captain, "You'd better give them a shout down there before you get committed." In other

words, before you proceed you need to know that the
river is open to—and including—your next manageable
hold-up spot. St. Louis to Chicago, Chicago to St. Louis,
this is like jumping from lily pad to lily pad.

. . .

When two moving tows, in adequate water, are passing, the captains say to each other, "See you on the 1,"
or "See you on the 2." Passing on the 1 always means
that both boats would turn to starboard to avoid collision. Two boats, meeting and passing on the 1, will go
by each other port to port. Therefore, passing on the 1
in opposite directions is different from passing on the
1 when overtaking. Passing on the 1 when overtaking is
to go by the other boat's starboard side. The stand-on
vessel, nearly always a vessel heading upstream, main-
tains everything as is. The action vessel maneuvers. If
you are learning this on the job, you may by now be up
a street in Peoria.

•

Another mantra, which I still write in chalk on the blackboard, is "A Thousand Details Add Up to One Impression."
It's actually a quote from Cary Grant. Its implication is that
few (if any) details are individually essential, while the details
collectively are absolutely essential.

What to include, what to leave out. Those thoughts are
with you from the start. While scribbling your notes in the
field, you obviously leave out a great deal of what you're looking at. Writing is selection, and the selection starts right there
at Square 1. When I am making notes, I throw in a whole lot of
things indiscriminately, much more than I'll ever use, but even
so I am selecting. Later, in the writing itself, things get down
to the narrowed choices. It's an utterly subjective situation.
I include what interests me and exclude what doesn't interest

me. That may be a crude tool but it's the only one I have. Broadly speaking, the word "interests" in this context has subdivisions of appeal, among them the ways in which the choices help to set the scene, the ways in which the choices suggest some undercurrent about the people or places being described, and, not least, the sheer sound of the words that bring forth the detail. It is of course possible to choose too much costume jewelry and diminish the description, the fact notwithstanding that, by definition in nonfiction writing, all the chosen items were of course observed.

If art is where you find it, you can find it in a remark by Cary Grant and you can find it in the strategy of Earl Blaik, the first college football coach to hire Vince Lombardi. Blaik coached at the U.S. Military Academy in an era when Army teams were undefeated. He amassed data from films (as everyone, of course, does now), and in those days films were made of actual film called celluloid. After being exposed, it had to be processed in a lab. West Point is fifty-five miles up the Hudson. The nearest lab was in Brooklyn. David Maraniss tells this story in *When Pride Still Mattered: A Life of Vince Lombardi* (Simon & Schuster, 1999, p. 107). Blaik sent the apprenticed Lombardi to Brooklyn to deliver Army football films and wait for them to be developed. Then, each week, his orders were to hurry back to West Point but only after stopping in Manhattan at the Waldorf-Astoria Towers and showing the football games to General Douglas MacArthur. The movies provided only a small percentage of the data Blaik routinely collected before preparing to face the next enemy. Maraniss:

Blaik's signature talent was using all this data to create something clean and simple. He had what Lombardi called "the great knack" of knowing what offensive plan to use against what defense and then "discarding the

immaterial and going with the strength." All the detailed preparations resulted not in a mass of confusing
statistics and plans, but in the opposite, paring away the
extraneous, reducing and refining until all that was left
was what was needed for that game against that team.
It was a lesson Lombardi never forgot. . . .

Possibly I could have used some coaching when I structured
Looking for a Ship. But it wouldn't have altered the result:

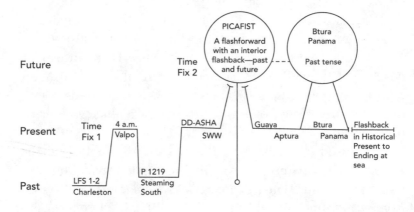

This was the weirdest ever, and in no way could serve as
even a faint suggestion of what an ideal structure should be—
that is, simple, straightforward, invisible. Despite its cunei-
form appearance, though, it functioned in a generally hidden
manner, but letters from readers did show up: "What happened after the ending?" "Did the ship ever make it to port?"
"What happened to the stowaways?" And so forth. The fact
that all such questions were answered in the text is not flatter-
ing to the attention attracted by the text.

In the beginning as well as the ending, I wanted to have
my cake and eat it too. I wanted the story of the voyage to begin
in total darkness on the ship's bridge at 4 a.m. in the southeast
Pacific Ocean off Valparaiso, and to be given the immediacy

of the present tense. As dawn began, the light would gradually reveal the appearance of the people who were talking. I also wanted to make clear at the outset the fact that my presence on that particular ship was the result of an essentially anonymous and absolutely random turn of union-hall chance, and to do that I needed to describe where I had travelled with a Second Mate who was looking for a ship. In a late part of the voyage—northbound, about a hundred miles offshore and approaching the Gulf of Panama—the ship went dead in the water. It wallowed in the swells. Two black balls were soon hoisted on the halyards of the uppermost mast—the universal statement "Not Under Command." This being a book whose deepest theme was the fading out and approaching doom of the U.S. Merchant Marine, I looked upon the engines' failure as a gift. I wanted the story to end with the ship lightly creaking, under the black balls, dead in the water.

This was 1988 and the structure was under total chronological control. It would be if I were writing it now. It began and ended with flashbacks. The cinematic present-tense lead on the dark bridge in Chilean waters was *preceded* by a past-tense account of how we came to be on that ship. To cover the points and events that came after the failure of the engines—the discovery of the stowaways in Balboa, dodging a tropical storm in the Caribbean, the discovery in Port Newark of a crack in the hull, visiting the captain at his home in Jacksonville and others of the crew in various cities—I had to think up ways to fix a block of time in the future.

Six years earlier, I was walking around in the Alps with a four-man patrol of Swiss soldiers. We had been together three weeks and were plenty compatible. Straying off-limits, not for the first time, we went into a restaurant called Restaurant. Military exercises were going on involving mortars and artillery up and down the Rhone Valley, above which the cantilevered Restaurant was fourteen hundred feet high. The soldiers had a two-way radio with which to receive orders, be given information, or report intelligence to the command post. They stirred their fondue with its antenna. They sent coded messages to the command post: "A PEASANT IN OBERWALD HAS SEEN FOUR ARMORED CARS COMING OUT OF ST. NIKLAUS AND HEADING FOR THE VALLEY." More fondue, then this: "TWO COMPANIES OF ENEMY MOTORIZED FUSILIERS HAVE REACHED RARON. ABOUT FIFTEEN ARMORED VEHICLES HAVE BEEN DESTROYED." And later this: "AN ATOMIC BOMB OF PETITE SIZE HAS BEEN DROPPED ON SIERRE. OUR BARRICADES AT VISP STILL HOLD. THE BRIDGES OF GRENGIOLS ARE SECURE. WE ARE IN CONTACT WITH THE ENEMY."

Setting down a pencil and returning to the fondue, I said to myself, "There is my ending." Like the failed engines on the ocean, the petite A-bomb was a gift to structure. Ending pieces is difficult, and usable endings are difficult to come by. It's nice when they just appear in appropriate places and times.

After the tow rig ran aground, the river pilot Mel Adams said, "When you write all this down, my name is Tom Armstrong."

I always know where I intend to end before I have much begun to write. William Shawn once told me that my pieces were a little strange because they seemed to have three or four endings. That surely is a result of preoccupation with structure. In any case, it may have led to an experience I have sometimes had in the struggle for satisfaction at the end. Look back upstream. If you have come to your planned ending and it doesn't seem to be working, run your eye up the page and the page before that. You may see that your best ending is somewhere in there, that you were finished before you thought you were.

People often ask how I know when I'm done—not just when

I've come to the end, but in all the drafts and revisions and substitutions of one word for another how do I know there is no more to do? When am I done? I just know. I'm lucky that way. What I know is that I can't do any better; someone else might do better, but that's all I can do; so I call it done.

Editors & Publisher

Robert Gottlieb replaced William Shawn as the editor of *The New Yorker* in 1987. If eccentricity was a criterion for the job, Bob was qualified. At one point, he had a toaster in his office that erupted two slices of plastic toast every hour on the hour. In the longest conversation I ever had with him, the toast popped up three times. It was late in the day and I missed as many trains. Bob knew how to listen, but the conversation was primarily monologue and had to do with his role in "saving *The New Yorker.*" He was not all plastic toast. Prompt and clear in reaction to manuscripts, he knew what he was publishing and was smarter than most writers, certainly this one. He had edited books for thirty years and been editor-in-chief of Simon & Schuster and Alfred A. Knopf. In his time at *The New Yorker*, I once submitted a piece that was almost eighty thousand words long. The following morning, he called to discuss it, rendering me speechless. To read eighty thousand words would take me two weeks. Maybe two months. When Gottlieb said he had read the manuscript, I didn't believe him; but then he analyzed two lengthy set pieces and their role in the over-all structure, told me where the scientific descriptions were and were not clear to him, and listed changes I might make to enhance the composition.

He was just as swift with "Looking for a Ship," but one item stopped him from the day I turned it in until "Looking for a Ship" appeared in *The New Yorker* nine months later. I had gone to Miami, Cartagena, Balboa, Buenaventura, Guayaquil, Callao, and Valparaiso on the merchant ship Stella Lykes, and had written sixty thousand words, of which Gottlieb was buying all but one. It had come out of the mouth of a sailor named John Shephard, who said, "It's a rough life. Rough life. Go ashore, you spend your money, get kicked in the tail. Plenty of friends till the money runs out. A seaman smells like a rose when he's got money, but when he has no money they say, 'Motherfucker, get another ship.'"

In the family of recoiling words included in *The New Yorker* for the first time, "motherfucker" had yet to be born. "Fuck" was alive but barely. John Cheever had agreed to delete it from a story published in the nineteen-fifties, in a tradition of compliance that extended to and beyond Alice Munro in 1980. During all that time, the editor of *The New Yorker* was William Shawn, who pluralized himself in the quiet expression "not for us." If he thought a euphemism was possible, Shawn would ask for one.

Writing a humor piece in the nineteen-sixties, Calvin Trillin imagined a maternity-dress shop called Mother Jumpers.

"Oh, no, not for us."

As Trillin has recounted in public and in print, he mentioned to Mr. Shawn that Mother Jumpers "was itself a euphemism."

"Yes, well, not for us."

The cartoonist Lee Lorenz, the art editor of *The New Yorker* for twenty years, was of the opinion that the magazine had "a somewhat undeserved reputation for prudishness." In a collection he compiled in homage to George Booth and to

Booth's herded cats and cross-eyed dogs, Lorenz wrote, "During the social upheavals of the sixties, while other publications were gleefully replacing the asterisks in s**t and f**k, the magazine stuck to its tradition of avoiding 'street language.' More than anything else, this attitude flowed from Shawn's reluctance to seem 'trendy.'"

If you want to meet ten different William Shawns, read Lee Lorenz, Lillian Ross, Allen Shawn, James Thurber, Roger Angell, Ved Mehta, Renata Adler, Brendan Gill, Garrison Keillor, and the book in your hand. I don't think trendiness was uppermost among Shawn's concerns when a "motherfucker" was trying to infiltrate his magazine. Mr. Shawn—this one-man "we," who would not accept advertising for cigarettes, or, in some instances, genital-contact clothing—was more than prepared to see Trillin's Mother Jumpers go off to another magazine, as he had been when he was said to have turned down Philip Roth's "Goodbye, Columbus," because a character mentioned a diaphragm.

Sara Lippincott, in a short piece written in the nineteen-seventies, tried a variant of "Use it or lose it," the Cialis of its time. Shouting from her bicycle at a New York bus driver, she said, "Move it or lose it!" Even that left Mr. Shawn blushed out. In his magazine, he was having none of it. "Why?" she asked him. Actually, she had no idea whence the expression derived. Shawn dodged her question. She asked again. He reddened and wouldn't tell her.

In the same long-gone era, however, Shawn accepted "ram it" in a piece by Trillin about Lester Maddox, the Governor of Georgia, who said publicly that "the federal government could take its education money and 'ram it.'" Shawn at first asserted that no such ramming was going to occur in *The New Yorker*. Trillin thought of leaving the magazine if Shawn did not relent. "What he was telling me . . . was that I had to stop listening when the other reporters were allowed to keep listening, and I didn't know if I could do that. Finally, he said he'd think about it overnight."

Next morning, Shawn called the writer and addressed him with a characteristic formality that would never change. Very softly, he said, "Hello, Mr. Trillin. How are you? Is this a convenient time to talk?"

Stet "ram it."

This was like the floating bits of vegetation that fifteenth-century navigators encountered a hundred miles from unplotted continents. At *The New Yorker*, euphemisms would someday fade. Someday, yes. But not by 1974, six years after "ram it," when I went into the insemination of quarter horses in contrast to the eroticism of Thoroughbreds. Try to imagine the reddening Mr. Shawn reading a manuscript that included this, and meanwhile forget about looking for it in the archives of the Shawn *New Yorker*:

Go Man Go stands at stud at Buena Suerte Ranch, in Roswell, New Mexico, his life an apparent idyll. Firm white fences surround his private paddock. His name is writ in gold on his private barn beside his own demarcated pastures. When the time comes for him to serve his purpose, though, he is led around to the clinic, where a group of mares has been prepared by teaser stallions. Handlers—halters in hand—hold the mares and hold the teasers. A teaser is not restrained as he moves close to a mare. He nuzzles her. He rubs against her. He makes deep sexual sounds. His heart pounds. His blood courses. Her blood courses, too. Nostrils flaring, he tries to mount. Forcefully, he is pulled down and away. He is dragged off to a corral. The mare has ovulated and is ready. Teaser stallions do not last long. In a matter of months, they break down psychologically.

Now, with fourteen or so mares teased up, Go Man Go is brought to the scene. He will not cover one love in a pasture, but fourteen mares in a clinic. One of them is presented to him and, without preliminaries, he mounts. A vet stands beside him. At the ultimate moment before penetration, the vet diverts Go Man Go into an artificial vagina. A heavy leather tube, lined with plastic, it is about two feet long and has a suitcase handle. In its outer walls are two valves, one for compressed air and the other for water heated to a hundred and sixty-seven degrees. Injected hot water bubbles with air, giving Go Man Go a sense of grand reception. "He doesn't know what is happening," the vet explains. "He thinks he is inside the mare."

A bottle in the artificial vagina catches the sperm and semen, which are immediately placed in a spectrometer. Fifty million sperm are counted off, and syringed into a teased-up mare. Fifty million more go into the next mare. One ejaculation will more than cover the entire group. Go Man Go is led back to his private pasture, dragging behind him his shattered metaphor: Go Man Go, standing at stud.

And not by 1975, needless to say, when I had paddled a hundred and fifty miles through the North Maine Woods in bark canoes with, among others, Henri Vaillancourt, the man who had made the canoes, using only an axe, an awl, a crooked knife, and a froe, sewing the hulls snug with the split roots of black spruce and other evergreens. He proved to be as headstrong in the woods and on the water as he was artful and deliberate in his shop, and he managed the trip as if he were the owner-skipper of a bireme. The last six miles were southeast-to-northwest over Caucomgomoc Lake, which is two miles wide, and when we came out of Ciss Stream and reached the lake we faced a headwind so strong that it was sinking deep troughs between high waves from which spray curled up like smoke. Vaillancourt dictated that we ignore this forbidding condition and cross the lake. We proceeded on. Scarcely a hundred yards northwest, the low-freeboard canoes were shipping water, and Vaillancourt's bowman, Warren Elmer, whose wariness of Vaillancourt's judgment had amplified day by day, now turned and bellowed at him, "You fucking lunatic, head for the shore!"

Fuck, fucker, fuckest; fuckest, fucker, fuck. In all my days, I had found that four-letter word—with its silent "c" and its quartzite "k"—more shocking than a thunderclap. My parents thought it was a rhetorical crime. Mr. Shawn actually seemed philosophical about its presence in the language, but not in his periodical. My young daughters, evidently, were in no sense as burdened as he was. Or as I was. Or as their grandparents were. In the car in their middle-school years, they batted that word between the back and front seats as if they were playing Ping-Pong. Driving, and hearing those words reach a critical mass, I once spontaneously bellowed (in an even-tempered, paternal way), "Fuck fuck fuck fuck fuck fuck fuck fuck—I can say it, too!"

Well, maybe in a car, but not in *The New Yorker*, not in 1975, and I didn't need to be told. I had been writing for the magazine for a dozen years. There were no alternatives like "f—" or "f**k" or "[expletive deleted]," which sounds like so much gravel going down a chute. If the magazine had employed such devices, which it didn't, I would have shunned them. "F-word" was not an expression in use then, and the country would be better off if it had not become one. So Warren Elmer said "fucking" on Caucomgomoc Lake, but the quote in *The New Yorker* was "You God-damned lunatic, head for the shore!"

1980. Onward and no change of altitude. For example, in

the last issue of that year, a line disappeared from Alice Munro's "The Turkey Season," and the gap was ficused over.

Munro in manuscript, presumably, for this is what appeared when "The Turkey Season" was collected in her book *The Moons of Jupiter*:

> He said he had got sick of it, though, and quit.
> What he said was, "Yeah, fuckin' boats, I got sick of that."
> Language at the Turkey Barn was coarse and free, but this was one word never heard there.

The New Yorker:

> He said he had got sick of it, though, and quit.
> Language at the Turkey Barn was coarse and free, but in telling us this Brian used an expression that is commonplace today but was not so then.

Seven years later, in the last months of Shawn's editorship, the soap sank at Procter & Gamble.

Trillin turned in a piece in which a financially beleaguered Nebraska farmer blamed his troubles on "the Goddam fuckin' Jews!" Trillin:

> I said that I felt I had to talk to Mr. Shawn about the quote, which was vital to my story, although I knew he had a lot on his plate and I wasn't going to get on my high horse if he said no. Mr. Shawn asked about the possibility of a euphemism. I told him that the quote was from a state-police transcript. We talked about other options for a while, and finally he said, "Just go ahead and use it." I mumbled something and backed slowly

out of the office, thinking that if I made an abrupt move
he might change his mind.

Into this milieu strode Bob Gottlieb, and when "Looking
for a Ship" went to press he was three years into the job. Here
and there in the piece were various shits and fucks, but they
did not preoccupy him. The vocabulary of the sailor John
Shephard still did preoccupy him: "Motherfucker, get another
ship."

On the day that the piece was to close, Bob called to ask if
I would come see him in his office. I loved going to his office.
Not just for the toaster. He kept part of his purse collection
there. He asked if I might think it advisable to reconsider the
sailor's word.

Shephard didn't reconsider it, I responded. How could I?
Bob said it was possible.

I said I preferred things as they were.

Bob leaned over a bright-yellow four-inch Post-it pad and
in big black letters wrote MOTHERFUCKER on it with a
Magic Marker. He was wearing an open-collared long-sleeved
shirt. He stuck the Post-it on the shirt pocket. He said he
would call me again later in the day.

I went back to my cell. Oddly, there was another brief passage in "Looking for a Ship" that might have concerned him,
but he made no comment, ever, and—who knows—may not
have thought it over. It dealt with tedium, and the yearning of
people who go to sea to get off the sea.

Here by free will, and (in most cases) with histories
behind them of decades on the sea, these people act
like prisoners making "X"s on a wall. I was to hear Jim
Gossett say to William Kennedy one morning, "Peewee,
we're under fifty days now. Forty-nine to go." This brought
to mind graffiti I had seen on the State of Maine, the

training ship of the Maine Maritime Academy. As part of the curriculum, students spend two summers on the State of Maine. The graffiti said, "Only 13 more MFD's, only 12 more MFD's, only 11 more MFD's," and so on down a toilet stall. The "D" stood for "day." To me it seemed a strange thing for someone to write who was going to college to go to sea. But no professional mariner would fail to understand it.

Off and on that day, Gottlieb walked the halls of the magazine wearing his MOTHERFUCKER Post-it as if it were a name tag at a convention. He looked in at office after office and loitered in various departments. He drew a blush here, a laugh there, startled looks, coughs, frowns. He gave writers moments of diversion from their writing. He gave editors moments to think of something other than writers. He visited just about everybody whose viewpoint he might absorb without necessarily asking for opinions. In the end, he called on me. He said *The New Yorker* was not for "motherfucker."

•

I was very lucky to come into *The New Yorker* when I did, its vocabulary notwithstanding. My first piece was in 1963, but it was generically a memoir, and short, a "casual" in the magazine's terminology, processed by the fiction department although it was fact. The piece that changed my existence came two years later, and was a seventeen-thousand-word profile of Bill Bradley, who was a student at Princeton. Shawn edited the piece himself, as he routinely did with new writers of long fact, breaking them in, so to speak, but not exactly like a horse, more like a baseball mitt. For a week or so before the press date, we met each day and went through galleys from comma to comma, with an extra beat for a semicolon. One point he was careful to make several times was that he was not interested

in buying pieces that "sound like *The New Yorker.*" I imagine
he was referring to the first-person plurals of The Talk of the
Town (as Talk was written then), because the signed pieces he
was publishing were not homogeneous. Nobody was going to
look at an unlabeled swatch of S. J. Perelman and think it was
written by Hannah Arendt. Now and again, Mr. Shawn said
things that were most encouraging to a fretful, not to say neu-
rotic, unconfident writer. He had had a lot of practice. He was
fifty-seven when I met him. When he turned seventy-nine, he
would still be *The New Yorker*'s editor. Among the varied forms
of writing that regularly appeared in the magazine, his own
greatest interest seemed to lie in the potentialities and possibilities of long nonfiction.

I wasn't aware of any of that before 1965. There was no
masthead, and I had never heard of him. Like most readers, I
thought *The New Yorker* was put together by some sort of en-
lofted tribunal, a consortium of editors "we." I had just wanted
since high school to see something of mine in *The New Yorker*,
and I had been continually rejected by *The New Yorker* until
I was in my thirties. And now I was sitting nineteen floors up
in an old building on Forty-third Street in a nondescript room
with a polite and formal small bald man talking three-two
zones, blind passes, reverse pivots, and the setting of picks.
The defensive structures and offensive moves had been unknown to him, and soon he would forget them, but this week
he wanted to understand them and passionately cared that
they were clear. For some reason—nerves, what else?—I had
forgotten to find a title before submitting the piece. Editors of
every ilk seem to think that titles are their prerogative—that
they can buy a piece, cut the title off the top, and lay on one
of their own. When I was young, this turned my skin pink
and caused horripilation. I should add that I encountered
such editors almost wholly at magazines other than *The New
Yorker*—*Vogue, Holiday, The Saturday Evening Post.* The title

is an integral part of a piece of writing, and one of the most important parts, and ought not to be written by anyone but the writer of what follows the title. Editors' habit of replacing an author's title with one of their own is like a photo of a tourist's head on the cardboard body of Mao Zedong. But the title missing on the Bill Bradley piece was my oversight. I put no title on the manuscript. Shawn did. He hunted around in the text and found six words spoken by the subject, and when I saw the first *New Yorker* proof the piece was called "A Sense of Where You Are."

I have been grateful for that for more than fifty years, but it did not make me any less wary of Shawn. About nonfiction titles, he had a set of basic prejudices that he presented as clauses in the constitution of the magazine. The name of the subject shall not be the title, for example, even if the subject is oranges, as was the case in the second long piece I handed in to him, my first as a staff writer. I called it "Oranges." That was the topic. What else did anyone need to know? Mr. Shawn took "Oranges" off the top and set up a proof called "Golden Lamps in a Green Night." Yes. You are not George Booth's dog. Your sight lines have converged on Shawn's title. He took it from Andrew Marvell's "Song of the Emigrants in Bermuda," which was quoted in the text. After I went to pieces, Mr. Shawn mercifully picked them up as "Oranges."

A couple of years later, after I turned in a piece I called "The Crofter and the Laird," Mr. Shawn again invoked the no-subjects-as-titles clause, and this time his solution was so unintrusive and touching that I felt defenseless. It ran in *The New Yorker* as "The Island of the Crofter and the Laird."

He wasn't all commas and quirks. He said definitive things. When I asked him if I could do a piece on oysters, he said, slowly and softly, "No. That is reserved, in a general way, for another writer."

"Another writer" was as close as he would ever come to

naming another writer in a conversation with another writer. Shawn was the hub of a bicycle wheel and his writers were the spokes. He kept them separate, stiffened, discrete—connected to him but not to one another. One rare and reckless time, speaking to me in low and confidential tones, he mentioned "facile writers" (not, of course, by name) and the price that facile writers pay for their facility, and the suspicions that accrue to their velvet prose, and so on until I found myself hoping that he thought my own work was as rough as a shingle beach. If you were male, he called you Mister. "Hello, Mr. Singer. How are you? Is this a convenient time to talk?" He was never more familiar than that. The formality seemed practical to me. It's easier to get rid of someone you call Mister. Think how much harder it would be to fire someone you were calling Sandy. If you were female, Mr. Shawn called you Miss or Mrs. He was born in 1907.

Two highly germane anecdotes about William Shawn and food—one concerning caribou in Alaska, the other about animals dead on the road in Georgia—have appeared in my book *Silk Parachute* and are quoted here:

Soon after the Alaska Native Claims Settlement Act was passed, in 1971, which resulted in the reorganization of Alaskan land on a vast and complex scale, I developed a strong desire to go there, stay there, and write about the state in its transition. When I asked William Shawn if he would approve and underwrite the project, his response was firm and negative. Why? Not because it was an unworthy subject, not because *The New Yorker* was over budget, but because he didn't want to read about any place that cold. He had a similar reaction to Newfoundland ("Um, uh, well, uh, is it cold there?"). Newfoundland, like Florida, is more than a thousand miles below the Arctic Circle, but Mr. Shawn shivered at the thought of it. I never went to work in Newfoundland, but, like slowly dripping water, I kept mentioning Alaska until at last I was in Chicago boarding Northwest 3.

The first long river trip I made up there was on the Salmon and the Kobuk, on the south slope of the Brooks Range. At some point, I learned and noted that the forest Eskimos of that region valued as a great delicacy the fat behind a caribou's eye. Pat Pourchot, of the federal Bureau of Outdoor Recreation (in recent years Alaska's commissioner of natural resources), had organized the river trip and collected the provisions. Pourchot's fields of special knowledge did not include food. For breakfast, he brought along a large supply of Pop-Tarts encrusted with pink icing and filled with raspberry jam. This caused me, in the manuscript ultimately delivered to the magazine, to present from the banks of the Kobuk River a philosophical choice:

> Lacking a toaster, and not caring much anyway, we eat them cold. They invite a question. To a palate without bias—the palate of an open-minded Berber, the palate of a travelling Martian—which would be the more acceptable, a pink-icinged Pop-Tart with raspberry filling (cold) or the fat gob from behind a caribou's eye?

There was in those days something known as "the Shawn proof." From fact-checkers, other editors, and usage geniuses known as "readers," there were plenty of proofs, but this austere one stood alone and seldom had much on it, just isolated notations of gravest concern to Mr. Shawn. If he had an aversion to cold places, it was as nothing beside his squeamishness in the virtual or actual presence of uncommon food. I had little experience with him in restaurants, but when I did go to a restaurant with him his choice of entrée ran to cornflakes. He seemed to look over his serving flake by flake to see if any were moving. On the Shawn proof beside the words quoted above, he had written in the wide, white margin—in the tiny letters of his fine script—"the pop tart."

•

So I have no idea by what freakishness of inattention Mr. Shawn had approved my application, a few years earlier, to go around rural Georgia with a woman who collected, and in many cases ate, animals dead on the road. She actually had several agendas, foremost of which was that she—Carol Ruckdeschel— and her colleague Sam Candler in the Georgia Natural Areas Council were covering the state in quest of wild acreages that might be preserved before it was too late. Under this ecological fog, Mr. Shawn seems not to have noticed the dead animals, let alone thought of them as anybody's food, but I was acutely conscious from Day 1 of the journey and Day 1 of the writing that my first and perhaps only reader was going to be William Shawn. It shaped the structure, let me tell you. Where to begin? With the weasel we ate the first night out? Are you kidding, I asked myself, and did not need to wait for the answer. This was an episodic narrative of eleven hundred miles—embracing an isolated valley in the Appalachian north and Cemocheckobee Creek, in the far south—and I could start in the shrewdest possible place in the structure that was to be shaped like a nautilus through chronological flashback. Where to begin? Near Hunger and Hardship Creek, on the Swainsboro Road, in Emanuel County, we had come upon a dying turtle— a snapping turtle. There had been a funny scene with a sheriff who tried to shoot the turtle at point-blank range and missed. A turtle is not a weasel. Snapping turtles are not unknown to commercial soupmakers. Weighing a snapping turtle against weasels and water moccasins did not require consultation. The scene on the trip that had followed the turtle was a stream-channelization project—no food for squeamishness there. And after the turtle and the channelization I could go off into the biography of the central figure (Carol Ruckdeschel) and I'd have managed what turned out to be eight thousand words of a Shawn-wise beginning before I had to start over and eat that weasel.

I turned in the manuscript and went for a five-day walk in my own living room. The phone rang.

"Hello."

"Hello, Mr. McPhee. How are you?" He spoke in a very light, very low, and rather lilting voice, not a weak voice, but diffident to a spectacular extent for a man we called the iron mouse.

"Fine, thank you, Mr. Shawn. How are you?"

"Fine, thank you. Is this a good time to be calling?"

"Oh, yes."

"Well, I liked your story. . . . No. I didn't like your story. I could hardly read it. But that woman is closer to the earth than I am. Her work is significant. I'm pleased to publish it."

Carol measured the weasel. She traced him on paper and fondled his ears. His skull and skin would go into the university's research collection.

As a research biologist, she gathered skulls and pelts for Georgia State University, whose students in their labs wore them out so quickly that they needed frequent replacement.

With a simple slice, she brought out a testicle; she placed it on a sheet of paper and measured it. Three-quarters of an inch. Slicing smoothly through the weasel's fur, she began to remove the pelt. Surely, she worked the skin away from the long neck. The flesh inside the pelt looked like a segment of veal tenderloin. "I lived on squirrel last winter," she said. "Every time you'd come to a turn in the road, there was another squirrel. I stopped buying meat. I haven't bought any meat in a year, except for some tongue. I do love tongue." While she talked, the blade moved in light, definite touches. "Isn't he in perfect shape?" she said. "He was hardly touched. You really lose your orientation when you start skinning an animal that's been run over by a Mack truck."

"Fine, thank you, Mr. Shawn. How are you?"

Carol put the weasel on the tines of a long fork and roasted it over the coals. "How do you like your weasel?" Sam asked me. "Extremely well done," I said. Carol sniffed the aroma of the roast. "It has a wild odor," she said. "You *know* it's not cow. The first time I had bear, people said, 'Cut the fat off. That's where the bad taste is.' I did, and the bear tasted just like cow. The next bear, I left the fat on." The taste of the weasel was strong and not unpleasant. It lingered in the mouth after dinner. The meat was fibrous and dark.

•

In discussing a long fact piece, Mr. Shawn would say, often enough, "How do you know?" and "How would you know?" and "How can you possibly know that?" He was saying clearly enough that any nonfiction writer ought always to hold those questions in the forefront of the mind.

In a ruminative, digressive way, he once remarked that he thought young writers were "taking longer to find out what kinds of writers they are," and he could think of no explanation. There was practical depth in those words alone, though. The writing impulse seeks its own level and isn't always given a chance to find it. You can't make up your mind in a Comp

Lit class that you're going to be a Russian novelist. Or even an American novelist. Or a poet. Young writers find out what kinds of writers they are by experiment. If they choose from the outset to practice exclusively a form of writing because it is praised in the classroom or otherwise carries appealing prestige, they are vastly increasing the risk inherent in taking up writing in the first place. It is so easy to misjudge yourself and get stuck in the wrong genre. You avoid that, early on, by writing in every genre. If you are telling yourself you're a poet, write poems. Write a lot of poems. If fewer than one work out, throw them all away; you're not a poet. Maybe you're a novelist. You won't know until you have written several novels.

I spent my teen-age years and well beyond them worrying about what sort of writer, if any sort of writer, I might become. I wrote in many genres in college, including poetry, showing such originality that after my friend George Garrett published some excellent free verse called "Fire Engine" I soon offered the *Nassau Literary Magazine* a short, stubby poem called "Fire Plug." Parody was not my intention, any more than plagiarism was my intention when I wrote of the tower of a ski jump that it swayed in the wind like readers of the *Boston Evening Transcript*. I was nineteen years old. Young writers generally need a long while to assess their own variety, to learn what kinds of writers they most suitably and effectively are, and every bit of that is what Shawn was encapsulating when he said the process seemed to be lengthening through time. Lengthening since when? He must have meant the nineteen-thirties, when he was a young editor. The process seemed very long in the fifties and sixties. In my case, after some television plays and who knows what, fictions became far between. I became completely absorbed with long nonfiction. The degree of difficulty in all forms of writing is high, and this was no picnic, but at least it felt right for me, as other forms did not. I have long thought that Ben Jonson summarized the process when he said, "Though a man be more prone and able for one kind of writing than another, yet he must exercise all." Gender aside, I take that to be a message to young writers.

Art is where you find it. Good writing is where you find it. Fiction, in my view, is much harder to do than fact, because the fiction writer moves forward by trial and error, while the fact writer is working with a certain body of collected material, and can set up a structure beforehand. It is sometimes said that the line between fiction and nonfiction has become blurred. Not in this eye, among beholders. The difference between the two is distinct. Curious this: "Fiction must stick to facts, and the truer the facts the better the fiction—so we are told." Virginia Woolf, *A Room of One's Own*.

Mr. Shawn was in the class of leaders who see no succession, like certain dictators, publishers, headmasters. Yet of course, as he advanced in years, the question of what would happen next grew around him like a rind. He reacted with stratagem. In the mid-nineteen-seventies, at least ten years before he actually retired and fifty before he meant to retire, he called me (as he did many other writers) and said he would like to try spreading some of his usual functions, implying but stopping short of saying that retirement was what he had in mind. From now on, he said, I would be dealing less with him about editorial matters than with Mr. Bingham. When something came up, I was to call Mr. Bingham. Only at certain times, Mr. Shawn said, would he be dealing directly with me; and those occasions would be, first, when I had an idea for a story and wished to propose it; second, when I had a completed manuscript to give to him; and third, when the story went to press.

Across his last decade as editor, he had almost as many dauphins as the French did in five hundred years. Or seemed to. And each of Shawn's heirs was never more than apparent.

As Confucius might say, You are what you can't become, but you can see to it, for a time, that no one becomes what you are. Shawn's successive designees were staff writers and staff editors. One by one, he raised them up, spotlighted them, and later found a reason (or seemed dismayed by a reason) to put them down. By and large, no two parties were offered the same explanation, and this resulted in misapprehensions, misunderstandings, enmities, and disappointments. Bystanders fell with the principals. This was not the only downside of an otherwise benevolent dictatorship, but it was probably the most cruel. He told Robert Bingham, for example, that Bingham would become *The New Yorker*'s editor; and Bingham, preparing himself mentally, lived with the expectation for a year or so before Shawn asked him to stop by when it was convenient, and told him that he was not to be the next editor, because, in the word Shawn used, Bingham was not of sufficient "character." An earlier dauphin had died. Ever after, Shawn invoked his memory when needed, saying, with a helpless look, that the deceased candidate had been the one person in modern history fully qualified to become the next editor.

Mr. Shawn understood the disjunct kinship of creative work—every kind of creative work—and time. The most concise summation of it I've ever encountered was his response to a question I asked him just before we closed my first *New Yorker* profile and he sent it off to press. After all those one-on-one sessions discussing back-door plays and the role of the left-handed comma in the architectonics of basketball—while *The New Yorker* magazine hurtled toward its deadlines—I finally said in wonderment, "How can you afford to use so much time and go into so many things in such detail with just one writer when this whole enterprise is yours to keep together?"

He said, "It takes as long as it takes."

As a writing teacher, I have repeated that statement to two generations of students. If they are writers, they will never forget it.

•

Shawn also recognized that no two writers are the same, like snowflakes and fingerprints. No one will ever write in just the way that you do, or in just the way that anyone else does. Because of this fact, there is no real competition between writers. What appears to be competition is actually nothing more than jealousy and gossip. Writing is a matter strictly of developing oneself. You compete only with yourself. You develop yourself by writing. An editor's goal is to help writers make the most of the patterns that are unique about them.

There are people who superimpose their own patterns on the work of writers and seem to think it is their role to force things in the direction they would have gone in if they had been doing the writing. Such people are called editors, and are not editors but rewriters. I couldn't begin to guess the number of onetime students of mine who have sent me printed articles full of notes in the margins telling me what the original said. An editor I know (not professionally) tells me that he sees this topic from the other side and most writers need what they get. He will never convince this writer. My advice is, never stop battling for the survival of your own unique stamp. An editor can contribute a lot to your thoughts but the piece is yours— and ought to be yours—if it is under your name.

Editors have come along who use terms like "nut graph"— as in "What this piece needs is a good nut graph"—meaning a paragraph close to the beginning that encapsulates the subject and why you are writing about it. That sort of structural formalism is a part of the rote methodology that governs the thought of people who don't have better ideas. Nut-graph moles have now and again infiltrated the subsummit levels of *The*

New Yorker. One mole told the editor C. P. Crow, in handing him an article to edit, that it was missing a nut graph, gratuitously adding, a bit later, that the author of the piece "sure knows how to tell a story."

Crow said, "So why don't you let him tell it."

Off and on, Crow edited pieces of mine for thirty years, and, after Bob Bingham died, was my principal editor for more than a decade. Crow was affable, likable, garrulous, thoughtful—yes. But with regard to the words in front of him he was a study in indiscernibility, not to say mystery and enigma. Did he like the piece? You weren't going to hear it from him. He had not bought the piece. The overarching editor had bought the piece. Had Crow even read the piece? Half a dozen times—as would gradually become clear in fine, emergent detail. Crow, who detectably loved food, was the garde-manger of the *New Yorker* process, reacting to the marginalia of grammarians, fact-checkers, first readers, second readers, closers, lawyers, and the Supreme Eyeshade, selecting the marginalia on a short spectrum from valid to imperative and passing them along to the author.

With Mark Singer and Ian "Sandy" Frazier, Crow spent a lot of time at my fishing shack, where he referred to Mark and Sandy—even when they were over sixty—as "the children." He once remarked of a dish I was preparing in advance that by afternoon it would be "dirty bacterial soup." I still wondered if he felt that way about some of my pieces of writing, but one day—out of nowhere, twenty-five years after editing something of mine about who knows what—he told me that he had just finished rereading it from a book on his shelf at home.

Editors are counselors and can do a good deal more for writers in the first-draft stage than at the end of the publishing process. Writers come in two principal categories—those who are overtly insecure and those who are covertly insecure—and they can all use help. The help is spoken and informal, and includes insight, encouragement, and reassurance with regard to a current project. If you have an editor like that, you are, among other things, lucky; and, through time, the longer the two of you are talking, the more helpful the conversation will be. At *The New Yorker*, I have had such luck, from those initial conversations with William Shawn to successive ones with Bob Bingham, Sara Lippincott, Pat Crow, John Bennet, and David Remnick, and also—in the shaping of books at Farrar, Straus and Giroux—with Harold Vursell, Tom Stewart, Patricia Strachan, Elisheva Urbas, Linda Healey, Natasha Wimmer, Jonathan Galassi, Alexander Star, and Paul Elie, himself an author of non-fiction books, whom I look up to as a writer and who, as an editor, seemed to care as much about my books as his own.

•

William Shawn and Roger W. Straus Jr., the president of Farrar, Straus and Giroux, were friends across the years, and in 1987 Roger actually hired Mr. Shawn, setting up an office for him in Union Square, after new owners of *The New Yorker* accomplished for Mr. Shawn, with respect to retirement, what he had no sincere interest in accomplishing for himself. The dissimilarity between Roger and Mr. Shawn could not be exaggerated. They were a pea and a prawn in a pod. Shawn grew up in the middle of the merchant class. Roger was born with a copper spoon in his mouth: the Kennecott Copper Corporation, American Smelting and Refining. His mother was a Guggenheim. Shawn was as shy as he was soft-spoken. Roger was a fountain of garrulity. Words came out of him so fast that he tried to economize by saying, at the end of every other sentence, "et cetera, et cetera, and so forth, and so on." If something was marvelous, it was "mawveless." His words wore spats.

He was a publisher, not an editor, but his conversational

attention to writers was, to say the least, voluminous. He nagged
a little. Oddly, it was he who would ask when was I going to
get my act together and finish some piece for *The New Yorker,*
while Shawn, in twenty-two years, never did. But mostly, with
Roger, it was just talk—in person from time to time, but mainly
on the telephone. I was a beginner when he began that. He
published my first book, in 1965, and he called maybe forty
times a year for something close to forty years.

Roger belonged to the Lotos Club, an institution housed
in a mansion on the Upper East Side and devoted to literature
and art. In the early nineteen-nineties, the club planned a
state dinner in Roger's honor and asked me and Tom Wolfe, as
FSG authors, to speak. When the day came, and my turn came,
I said, "I hope you don't mind if I speak from notes. In an
author-publisher relationship of nearly thirty years, this is the
first opportunity I have had to get some words in edgewise,
and I don't want to let even one of them get away. Last fall,
after I was invited to speak here on January 30th, Roger Straus
soon called me to say that this was entirely the club's idea,
et cetera, et cetera, and so forth, and so on, and definitely not
his idea. 'In fact,' he said, 'I told them I didn't think you were
very bright.' He said that he did not want me to feel any obliga-
tion whatsoever to him. There was no need for me to have to
come all the way in from Princeton. Et cetera, et cetera. And so
forth, and so on.

"I said, 'That's not the issue, Roger. That's not what we're
discussing. What I need to know is, Is it all right to say "Fuck
you" in the Lotos Club?'

"He said, 'I see the lines along which you are thinking. Of
course it's all right. It's perfectly all right. And, besides, you're
not a member.'"

When I was quite young, I was inadvertently armored for
a future with Roger Straus. My grandfather was a publisher.

My uncle was a publisher. The house was the John C. Winston Company, "Book and Bible Publishers," of Philadelphia, Pennsylvania, and on their list was the Silver Chief series, about a sled dog in the frozen north. That dog was my boyhood hero. One day, I was saddened to see in a newspaper that Jack O'Brien, the author of those books, had died. A couple of years passed. I went into high school. The publishing company became Holt, Rinehart & Winston, and my uncle Bob's office moved to New York. When I was visiting him there one day, a man arrived for an appointment, and Uncle Bob said, "John, meet Jack O'Brien, the author of *Silver Chief*." I shook the author's hand, which wasn't very cold. After he had gone, I said, "Uncle Bob, I thought Jack O'Brien died."

Uncle Bob said, "He did die. He died. Actually, we've had three or four Jack O'Briens. Let me tell you something, John. Authors are a dime a dozen. The dog is immortal."

As I have mentioned before, in various places and publications, Roger Straus would have understood not only my grandfather but also my great-grandfather Joseph Palmer, a farmer who had a mill pond and a sawmill on Doe Run, about thirty miles west of Philadelphia. He made, among other things, book boards—the hard parts of what are now called hardcover books. He sold them to Charles Ziegler, my great-uncle, who owned Franklin Bindery, and whose best customer was the John C. Winston Company. Winston claimed to publish more Bibles than anyone else in the world, and at the other end of their list was my grandfather's specialty, the hardcover equivalent of the newspaper extra. In 1912, he published a quickie on the Titanic while the bubbles were still numerous and the ice had yet to melt.

Being a publisher, my grandfather naturally kept a pair of pearl-handled .44-calibre Colt Peacemakers in a velvet-lined box in his study.

I dealt with Roger Straus without an agent. Contractual

negotiations took place in private conversation between us. I risked foolishness. I once asked Roger, "How much money am I losing as a result of not having an agent?" And he answered, "Not a whole hell of a lot."

One time, when he was contracting to publish a hefty hardcover book with my name on it as author, I asked him for an advance, and he said, "Fuck you." That is exactly what he said. Truth be told, though, the book was an amalgam of fragments of other books, for which he had long since paid advances.

He always said that he wanted to publish authors, not books. This principle contained not only an admirable loft but also a faint implication that if you had a dog you could bring it to the party. In 1968, when we talked about publishing what was to be my fifth book but first collection of miscellaneous pieces, I said to him, "This one isn't going to make a nickel. Collections never do. I'm grateful to you just for publishing it. Don't bother to pay me an advance."

"Nonsense," he said. "I'm your publisher. Of course I will pay you an advance. I insist." And he named a sum so low that I am somewhat shy to reveal it.

In fact, it was fifteen hundred dollars. The book was published in 1969. It did not do well over the counter. It took fourteen years to earn back the fifteen hundred dollars. Notice something, though: after all those years, it was in print. Commercially, that book could not have been a bigger dog if its title was *Remainder.* In conglomerate publishing, it would have vanished three weeks after it was published. But Roger kept it in print, as he kept all my books—marginal and otherwise, hardcover and soft—in print. When I cashed his checks, I could hear the tellers giggling as I walked away, but even in my Scottish core I really didn't care. Across the first decade of the twenty-first century, that ancient collection of miscellaneous pieces sold about seven hundred copies a year. A small figure. But for that book—for any trade book—forty-some years is an amazing longevity. Thanks entirely to its publisher. The dog is immortal.

At the Lotos Club, after telling some of those stories, I said, "Tom and I are here because Tom is the house eagle and I am the company mule. I say that with no false humility. I say it as plain fact. I would not know how to light a bonfire if some-one handed me the match. I write about geology. In a sense, I am selling rocks. In Union Square, I know a sucker who will buy them."

In 1975, I began teaching my course in factual writing at Princeton. Annually, until after the turn of the millennium, Roger drove down in his Mercedes and talked nonstop to the assembled students—et cetera, et cetera, and so forth, and so on—with a cumulative rate of repetition of four per cent. He repeatedly came to the course in a period when his health was inconvenienced by cancer. The students were always well pre-pared to interview him, but one question was enough. "Could you tell us about Aleksandr Solzhenitsyn?" someone said. And Roger said, "Eighteen years ago, when I first started having serious intercourse with the big A . . ." and he was off and running for three hours of free association.

When *The New Yorker* appeared to Roger to be heading down some sort of tube, he came to my campus office and of-fered five independent book contracts aggregating a sum that would not impress a hedge-fund manager but might have im-pressed a literary agent had one been present—or, as I said at Roger's memorial service, in 2004 at the 92nd Street Y, "It was enough money, actually, to keep me alive until this moment, which Roger may have had in mind. I'm a little sorry that I am speaking at his service rather than he at mine, because it would have been a lot more entertaining the other way around. I used to try not to think about the possibility that some day the dialogue would end, the hundreds and hundreds of phone calls, the flying humor. He was there in my thirties, forties, fifties, and sixties, and was still leading me up the street on a leash when I entered my seventies. If he kept back money that he might have laid on me, I'm particularly happy about that now, because I'm sure he has it with him, and he'll need it."

Elicitation

If I'm in someone's presence and attempting to conduct an interview, I am wishing I were with Kafka on the ceiling. I'd much rather watch people do what they do than talk to them across a desk. I've spent hundreds of hours in the passenger seats of their pickups, often far from pavement, bouncing from scribble to scribble. Under a backpack, and hiking behind the environmentalist David Brower, I walked across the North Cascades, up and down the switchbacks, writing in a notebook. Even across a desk, an interviewee will sometimes talk so fast it's impossible to keep up—like Alan Hume, M.D., a surgeon in Waterville, Maine. Nothing was unforthcoming about Dr. Hume. He talked clearly, rapidly, volubly, and technically. Writing notes, I did my best to stay with him, but when he breezed into the biochemistry of the blood gases I was totally lost and turned him over to a Japanese machine.

Suppose you are in Vermont on a field trip with the world's ten or fifteen most knowledgeable Appalachian geologists. They gather around an outcrop, and soon an argument heats up about delaminated basements, welding batholiths, and controversial aspects of tectonostratigraphy. You are on the low side

of the learning curve and don't even know terrain from ter-
rane. What to do? Put a voice recorder on the outcrop.

"It has no fossil control!"

"It's a distal part of North America!"

You can read up later on what this means.

In the way that a documentary-film crew can, by its very
presence, alter a scene it is filming, a voice recorder can affect
the milieu of an interview. Some interviewees will shift their
gaze and talk to the recorder rather than to you. Moreover, you
may find yourself not listening to the answer to a question
you have asked. Use a voice recorder, but maybe not as a first
choice—more like a relief pitcher.

Whatever you do, don't rely on memory. Don't even imagine that you will be able to remember verbatim in the evening
what people said during the day. And don't squirrel notes in
a bathroom—that is, run off to the john and write surrepti-
tiously what someone said back there with the cocktails. From
the start, make clear what you are doing and who will publish
what you write. Display your notebook as if it were a fishing
license. While the interview continues, the notebook may serve
other purposes, surpassing the talents of a voice recorder. As
you scribble away, the interviewee is, of course, watching you.
Now, unaccountably, you slow down, and even stop writing,
while the interviewee goes on talking. The interviewee becomes nervous, tries harder, and spills out the secrets of a secret life, or maybe just a clearer and more quotable version of
what was said before. Conversely, if the interviewee is saying
nothing of interest, you can pretend to be writing, just to keep
the enterprise moving forward.

If doing nothing can produce a useful reaction, so can the
appearance of being dumb. You can develop a distinct advantage by waxing slow of wit. Evidently, you need help. Who
is there to help you but the person who is answering your questions? The result is the opposite of the total shutdown that

might have occurred if you had come on glib and omniscient. If you don't seem to get something, the subject will probably help you get it. If you are listening to speech and at the same time envisioning it in print, you can ask your question again, and again, until the repeated reply will be clear in print. Who is going to care if you seem dumber than a cardboard box? Reporters call that creative bumbling.

As a beginning reporter, I developed such behaviors while interviewing show-business people for *Time* magazine. Some of these assigned subjects were a great deal more difficult to manage than others, none simpler or more agreeable than Woody Allen. Odd as it seems now, so many years later, he came to *Time*, and up to my cubicle in Rockefeller Center. He was twenty-seven years old, and volunteered that he was a "latent heterosexual." He said he strongly wished to return to the womb—"anybody's." I described him in the piece as "a flatheaded, redheaded lemur with closely bitten fingernails and a sports jacket." He spoke of people who "perspire audibly." He said his father had been a factory worker but was replaced by a small gadget. His mother bought one. At the time of the interview, Woody Allen was working standup in a Greenwich Village night club. As a writer for TV comedians, he said, he had written twenty-five thousand gags in two years. The fact that he was telling some of them to me did not concern either of us.

On the difficulty scale, Jackie Gleason was at the other extreme. In 1961, his film *The Hustler*, with Paul Newman, came along, and seemed to mark a significant rejuvenation of Gleason's career, which had run a long course on television. When he agreed to be interviewed for a cover story, he was making another movie—*Requiem for a Heavyweight*, with Mickey Rooney and others, including the young Muhammad Ali, who was still Cassius Clay. When I attended the filming— in December, on Randalls Island, in the East River—the cast was huddled under the stadium in a cold, fog-shot, tubercular setting. Gleason's dressing room was a small house trailer. When he stepped aboard, it squished down half a foot and nearly capsized. Each day, for a couple of days, he invited me in and responded readily and patiently to questions. A day soon came, though, when—in a complete reversal of attitude—he threw me out. He said I worked for assassins. He said I was going to assassinate him. He nonetheless addressed me as Pal.

"Pal, it's all over."

When Gleason was not on Randalls Island, he went often to Jack & Charlie's '21', on West Fifty-second Street, with his other pals. At the time, these included Ralph Nelson, who was directing *Requiem for a Heavyweight*, David Susskind, who was producing it, and Mickey Rooney. These were the parties who described *Time* magazine as a tower of assassins. How do I know that? Gleason told me so. And he believed them—believed that he was being set up to be satirically cut down. He had a boozy reputation. One of the pals had said to him, "Jackie, they're going to make you look like a drunk fucking son of a bitch."

But they weren't. It would make no sense.

He was six years beyond *The Honeymooners*, his apex of stardom as a situation comedian on CBS. A comedy hour called *The Jackie Gleason Show*—on which he did skits as Reginald Van Gleason III, Fenwick Babbitt, and Rum Dum—had not brought comparisons with Laurence Olivier. But now, amazingly, he had risen anew as a first-rate actor in a Hollywood film. What we intended to say was something like this:

Minnesota Fats is played, curiously enough, by Jackie Gleason, and where audiences might have arrived expecting a million laughs from the most celebrated buffoon ever to rise through U.S. television, they leave with a single, if surprised, reaction: inside the master jester, there is a masterful actor. Gleason, the storied comedian,

egotist, golfer, and gourmand, mystic, hypnotist, boozer
and bull slinger, is now emerging as a first-rank star of
motion pictures.

On the telephone, I tried to suggest to Gleason that the
vector of my assignment was aimed in that direction, to which
he said, "So long, pal."

Two or three days later, he called and said he had been
thinking it over and I could return to the trailer on Randalls
Island. The resumed interviews went well there until he kicked
me out again. What had Mickey Rooney said this time? I didn't
need a transcript.

The on-again, out-again, off-again interview continued in
that way but actually made progress. Gleason was companion-
able and funny, and generally worked hard to give the most
complete and thoughtful reply he could to every question. Then
he called one morning, told me to stay away, and said it was
really over this time—done, finished.

A freelance cover artist—Russell Hoban—had been com-
missioned by *Time* to do an acrylic portrait of the subject. Ralph
Nelson, David Susskind, and Mickey Rooney had persuaded
Hoban to bring the painting to '21'. Hoban unwrapped it there
in front of Gleason and his advisory panel. True, the painting
did not seem destined for a Hallmark card, would not have
been mistaken for the work of Norman Rockwell. An unkind
observer could construe it to resemble the wax on a bottle in a
Calabrian restaurant. Words came forth in a virtual chorus.
"You see, Jackie? You see it now? They want to make you a
drunk fucking son of a bitch."

A day later, making one last try, I called him. He was back
at '21', and his pals were not there. I said I had not seen the
painting, had nothing to do with it, and as a writer meant to
celebrate him, purely and simply. There was no point in doing
anything else.

He said, "You're just a flunky, pal. You can tell me all that but it doesn't mean anything. You don't run *Time* magazine."

I told him he had that one right.

He said, "Who does run *Time* magazine?"

I said, "Otto Fuerbringer."

"Who is he?"

"The managing editor. Would you like to meet him?"

"Why not?"

"I'll ask him."

I went down a couple of corridors to a far corner of *Time*'s editorial floor. Fuerbringer was in his office. After I told him the situation, he got up and walked with me to the elevator bank. From the Time & Life Building, we walked two blocks north to Fifty-second, and east to '21'.

Gleason: "Who is in charge of *Time* magazine?"

Fuerbringer: "I am."

Gleason: "Who has the last word at *Time*?"

Fuerbringer: "I do."

Fuerbringer did not have a name like that because he was Caspar Milquetoast. He had a deceptively soft voice and a ready smile, but nothing made him flinch. Slowly, firmly, he cleared away the scent of Ralph Nelson, David Susskind, and Mickey Rooney. The cover painting and the cover story ran in the issue of December 29, 1961.

Location shooting had moved on from Randalls Island to Jack Dempsey's restaurant, on Broadway. Handed a copy of the magazine, Gleason asked for time out, sat alone at the bar, and slowly turned the pages. Greg Morrison, the film company's publicist, told me this a day later. Gleason spent at least half an hour turning pages and looking expressionlessly at what he was reading.

"If I didn't have an enormous ego and a monumental pride, how in hell could I be a performer?" he explains.

With something for everybody, he is kind, generous, rude
and stubborn, explosive, impulsive, bright and mischie-
vous. He is an outgoing, flamboyant man to whom privacy
is sacred. Now he is snapping out wisecracks. Now he
is sitting alone, quietly unapproachable. He is too often
bored. He is a bad listener in general conversation and
a good one when acting. He has a great big kettledrum
laugh. He is afraid of airplanes and strangers. "He is all
fun and jazz until a stranger comes in," says a onetime
member of his staff. "Then he goes into that fat shell." . . .
He has a huge vocabulary, which sometimes slices into
the rough. "Don't misconcept this," he will say, or "That
guy is a man of great introspect." But his favorite ad-
jective is "beautiful," his favorite noun is "pal," and his
favorite phrase is "beautiful, pal, beautiful."

Gleason got up from the bar and went to Jack Dempsey's
telephone booth.
My phone rang. "Hello."
"Pal, I feel like two cents."
There were those who thought of him as a potential source
of a great deal more money than that. In 1962 or 1963—I
forget when—a man walked into the Gleason offices on West
Fifty-seventh Street, identified himself as "John McPhee," and
asked for a cash loan. Gleason was in Florida at a golf club. A
staff member telephoned him and told him what was happening. Gleason said to her, "Describe him."
She said, "Well, for one thing he's very tall."
Gleason said, "Call the police."

•

The interviews with Jackie Gleason were not recorded.
With my basic technology—a pencil and a lined four-by-six
notebook—I could keep up. He spoke at a clear and thoughtful

pace. Besides, like most people, he was not invariably interesting. Writing is selection. When you are making notes you are
forever selecting. I left out more than I put down.

Students have always asked what I do to prepare for interviews. Candidly, not much. At minimum, though, I think you
should do enough preparation to be polite. You would not have
wanted to ask Stephen Harper what he did for a living. Before, during, and after an interview, or a series of interviews,
do as much reading as the situation impels you to do. In the
course of writing, you really find out what you don't know,
and you read in an attempt to get it right. Nonetheless, you
get it wrong, especially if you are an innumerate English major
and you are writing about science. After an interview with
Robert Hargraves, a Princeton geologist who grew up in South
Africa, I attempted a description of maar-diatreme volcanoes,
which bring carbon up from the mantle with such velocity that
carbon in its densest form freezes as diamonds in the volcanic
neck. It is journalistic custom—essentially a rule—that you
don't show a manuscript to the subject. In many situations, ego
is too likely to spoil the transaction, not to mention a subject's
attempts to massage the text. But science, for me, is the exception that probes the rule. I have never published anything
on a science that has not been vetted by the scientists involved. Robert Hargraves read about the maar-diatreme vol-
cano and said I had it half right. A couple of days later, I
returned to him with a fresh version, which he said was three-
quarters right. A few days after that, I asked him to look
again. This time, he said, "I don't see anything wrong here."
I felt as if he had awarded me a Ph.D., the "D," perhaps, for
the synonym for subpar intelligence.

Not everybody is as detached as Robert Hargraves or as
savvy as Jackie Gleason. Plenty of people who are willing to
talk are not at the same time sensing what the effect of the

eventual piece will be. The presence of the open notebook, and the formality of being advised about what is going to happen and where, is not enough. It is true that some people I have written about—Thomas P. F. Hoving, of the Metropolitan Museum, comes readily to mind—are so cognizant of the piece of writing taking shape that they all but supply the commas. Hoving is at one end of a spectrum, and the other end is populous. So the writer has responsibility to be fair to the subject, who trustingly and perhaps unwittingly delivers words and story into the writer's control. Some people are so balanced, self-possessed, and confident that they couldn't care less what some ragmaker says about them, but they are in a minority among people who put their lives in your hands.

Of all the dimensions of the interview relationship, the most significant, for me, has been time. The daily journalist has to go out, get the story, and write it in one day, a feat that leaves me breathless and beggars all comparison with the time involved in my projects—four months in the New York City Greenmarkets, three weeks with a flying game warden, two weeks with a Nevada brand inspector, months at a time across three years of trips to Alaska. I have no technique for asking questions. I just stay there and fade away as I watch people do what they do.

In a question-and-answer piece in *The New York Times Book Review* for January 16, 1966, George Plimpton quoted Truman Capote claiming that he had trained himself to recall dialogue with such accuracy that he could interview people without a notebook or tape recorder, and then, hours later, write down verbatim what was said, his accuracy exceeding ninety per cent.

In 1991, when James Atlas was an editor at *The New York Times Magazine*, he wrote an article about—among other things—quotation marks and what is inside them. How much

is quoter, how much quotee? By way of example, Atlas quotes
Boswell quoting Johnson at a dinner party. Johnson, between
bites: "It is so far from being natural for a man and woman to
live in a state of marriage that we find all the motives which
they have for remaining in that connection and the restraints
which civilized society imposes to prevent separation are
hardly sufficient to keep them together." Atlas: "That's quite a
mouthful, even for a speaker with Johnson's verbal gifts." In
fairness to Boswell, Atlas went on to say, "Boswell was an assiduous note-taker; he would scribble a few lines, abridging
words—his 'portable soup,' he called it: 'a hint, such as this,
brings to my mind all that passed, though it would be barren
to anybody but myself.'" Anybody but Truman Capote, apparently, who didn't even need a soupspoon.

Once captured, words have to be dealt with. You have to
trim them and straighten them to make them transliterate
from the fuzziness of speech to the clarity of print. Speech and
print are not the same, and a slavish presentation of recorded
speech may not be as representative of a speaker as dialogue
that has been trimmed and straightened. Please understand:
You trim and straighten—take the "um"s, "uh"s, and "uh but
um"s out, the false starts—but you do not make it up.

Henri Vaillancourt, in whose bark canoes I travelled through
the North Maine Woods, liked the word "bummer." At least
fourteen hours a day, I was making notes, and Henri was saying
"bummer" at least sixty times an hour, or so it seemed. In any
case, my notes were nearly saturated with "bummer"s. Writing
the piece, I consciously removed two-thirds of them. After the
piece was published, I heard from strangers and friends alike
that no real-life human being would ever say "bummer" that
often.

And while we are on this subject, please let me indulge in
a parenthetical peeve, which has to do with the way in which
pronouns can infect sentences that contain interior quotes—

the pronouns apparently changing horses in midstream. To give just one random example: "He arrived at the pier, where he learned that 'my ship had come in.'" Whose ship? The author's ship? Try reading something like that before an audience or on an audio CD. It is factual and carefully punctuated, but it is no less awkward. I have attempted for forty years to get writing students to avoid such constructions, an endeavor that has resulted in serial failure.

In a 1991 decision, the Supreme Court, six to three, rebuffed Jeffrey Masson, a psychoanalyst who claimed libel in quotations attributed to him by Janet Malcolm, of *The New Yorker.* Justice Anthony M. Kennedy wrote the majority opinion. "In some sense, any alteration of a verbatim quotation is false," he said at one point. "But writers and reporters by necessity alter what people say, at the very least to eliminate grammatical and syntactical infelicities." Any reasonable "reader would understand the quotations to be nearly verbatim reports of statements made by the subject." Nota bene, Justice Kennedy said "at the very least," said "nearly verbatim," and said "by necessity alter." In other words, the reader of ordinary skill in the art understands what Sara Lippincott, of *The New Yorker,* used to call the dusting of quotes. Justice Kennedy called such practices "technical falsity."

Libel is not of any interest to me here, but in the course of the majority opinion, the court made points of considerable relevance to the general practice of nonfiction writing. If Kennedy and his five concurring confreres had wearied of law and sought work at a journalism school, I'd have been for giving them tenure. Or, as Linda Greenhouse put it in *The New York Times*, "The opinion by Justice Anthony M. Kennedy was greeted with widespread relief by lawyers representing the press. They said that the court had displayed a welcome sensitivity toward the practical problems that writers face in trying to capture the words of interview subjects. . . ."

The task could be daunting. George Herbert Walker Bush, the forty-first President of the United States, on January 10, 1992: "I think there were some differences, there's no question, and will still be. We're talking about a major major situation here. . . . I mean, we've got a major rapport—relationship of economics, major in the security, and all of that, we should not lose sight of." The commas and dashes of transcribers can be unequal to the task: "We look around the world and we see the darndest, most dramatic changes moving towards the values that—that have made this country the greatest, freedom, democracy, choice to do things—you know." Ibid., January 12, 1990. "And I guess with these cameras listening, be sure never to end your sentence with a—without—end a sentence with a preposition because it will be duly reported all across the country by these guardians of the . . ." Ibid., March 29, 1989. "Thank you all very much. And let me just say this, on a personal basis. I've screwed up a couple of times here and I'm very grateful for your assistance in straightening it out. God, I'd hate to have had some of those answers stand." Ibid., press conference, August 8, 1990.

Nor did the seed fall far from the bush.

Returning to Justice Kennedy: "Even if a journalist has tape recorded the spoken statement of a public figure, the full and exact statement will be reported in only rare circumstances" because of "the practical necessity to edit and make intelligible a speaker's perhaps rambling comments."

It is possible in managing a quote—not to say manipulating a quote—to present something that is both verbatim and false. In a book published in 1977, I said, "Alaska is a foreign country significantly populated with Americans." In a July, 2009, piece on Sarah Palin, *Time* magazine quoted the book, saying, "Alaska is a foreign country." And think what could happen to the following. It comes from public radio, and this is the quote in its entirety: "Republican Congressman Darrell Issa wants the heads of the panel to be forthcoming about their sources of information." A shorter sentence would still be a verbatim quote if someone were to stop at "panel."

Justice Kennedy also wrote, "In general, quotation marks around a passage indicate to the reader that the passage reproduces the speaker's words verbatim. They inform the reader that he or she is reading the statement of the speaker, not a paraphrase or other indirect interpretation by an author. By providing this information, quotations add authority to the statement and credibility to the author's work." And more: "Quotations allow the reader to form his or her own conclusions, and to assess the conclusions of the author, instead of relying entirely upon the author's characterization of her subject." Hear, hear. In complex situations, quotation, fairly handled, can help keep judgment in the eye of the beholder, and that is a deeper mission for a writer than crafting a sermon from a single point of view.

Indirect discourse is an excellent way to say what someone said and avoid the matter of verbatim quoting altogether. It is hard to be uncomfortable with indirect discourse. If a quote is something like "I'll be there prepared for anything at the first hint of dawn," and you think, for any reason, that it may have too much dust on it to be in the verbatim zone, get rid of the quotation marks and state it in indirect discourse (improving the logic while you're at it):

She said she would be there at the first hint of dawn, prepared for anything.

Is it wrong to assemble dialogue collected in three or four places and ultimately present it as having been spoken in a fifth location? I think so. Do you? I have gone back to people asking them to correct and sometimes amplify what they told me, and I have corrected and amplified the quotes but have

never changed the original venue. Would you call that imper-
missible? I wouldn't. Is it wrong to alter a fact in order to improve the rhythm of your prose? I know so, and so do you. If
you do that, you are by definition not writing nonfiction.

J. Anthony Lukas, in his author's note before *Common
Ground*, wrote: "This is a work of non-fiction. All its characters
are real. . . . Where I have used dialogue, it is based on the
recollection of at least one participant." At least one participant? Bob Woodward, in a note to the reader before *The
Commanders*, said: "Thoughts, beliefs and conclusions attributed to a participant come from that individual or from a
source who gained knowledge of them directly from that
person." In this manner, the rumble of conscientiousness makes
its way through time. I remember overhearing a feverishly
principled great journalist responding on the phone to an
editor or checker, and insisting that not one syllable in a piece
be changed for clarity or any other purpose. If, in the field of
conscientiousness, it is possible to go the extra mile, this was
the extra mile. "That is the quote!" the writer shouted. And
again, "That *is* the quote." As it happened, the quote had been
translated from Russian.

Norman Maclean called *A River Runs Through It* fiction,
and the word "fiction" appeared in the book's front matter. *A
River Runs Through It* was autobiographical fact in nearly all
aspects but one. For private reasons, the author had shifted
the site of his brother's murder and, being Norman Maclean,
considered that change and others quite enough fabrication to
disqualify the text as nonfiction.

•

Minders are watchdogs in coats and ties whose presence is a
condition for an interview. Corporations and federal agencies
deploy them. They are not exactly catalytic in the interview
process. Distractingly, they sometimes make notes. They will

even answer an interviewer's questions although their role is supposedly limited to observing and monitoring what is being said. Some have been described as "Saddam-style minders." I have been very lucky with minders, in large measure because for more than half a century I have successfully avoided them, with two innocuous exceptions. In 2004, I began a piece on the Sort—the vast, robotic, multilevel maze in Louisville, Kentucky, where UPS absorbs, shuffles, and redirects a million packages a day. To circumambulate the building would be a five-mile hike, and no one is going to do that, even with a minder. Numerous large brown-tailed airplanes nose up to the western side. The runways of Louisville International Airport are right there. Never would I have been permitted to drive around those bays and taxiways without a minder, let alone wander among the zipping packages on the endless conveyors inside, the drug-sniffing dogs. I actually spent a couple of weeks with my minder, who was unobtrusively present at nearly all the interviews I did there, involving many dozens of workers. His name was Travis Spalding. He grew up in West Point, Kentucky, on the Ohio River near Fort Knox. In no sense did he seem to think that I was trying to steal anybody's gold. On the weekend, when my time was my own, I went to Churchill Downs with him, his wife, his mother, and his father.

The other minder was provided in Omaha in 1995 by the Federal Bureau of Investigation. Through the agency's Materials Analysis Unit, about half of whose work is in geology, I had arranged to interview Special Agent Ronald Rawalt, a mineralogist and paleontologist who had performed a feat of geological espionage in Mexico that had essentially solved the murder of an American drug agent there. Rawalt's home and office were in North Platte, Nebraska. So, logically, fly to Denver and drive to North Platte. Right? Not so fast. Rawalt was instructed to meet me at 9 a.m. on January 24th in a room in the federal building in Omaha—two hundred and eighty miles from his home. When I went into the room, the minder was there. He was there for eight or nine hours, but, as it happened, not for the entire interview. Rawalt was talking petrology, mineralogy, crystallography, the solubility of quartz, and the exoscopic study of sands. I never learned the minder's name. It probably would not be fair to say that he went to sleep. He was quiet, though, and as evening settled in he departed. Rawalt talked on, and was still talking twelve hours after we had begun.

I had used a tape recorder throughout. Back home, as I was transcribing his narrative, I discovered that among the cassettes one had failed. Stunned, I called Rawalt, who asked what he had been saying at the end of the previous cassette and what he had said at the start of the one that followed. With a machine of his own, on his kitchen table, in North Platte, he narrated anew an indispensable part of the story. Rawalt paid for the postage, you did not.

One very foggy morning five years later, I was in my office on the Princeton campus, the phone rang, and the Council of the Humanities informed me that an F.B.I. agent had come in asking for me and had gone out again; his name was Rawalt and he was waiting in the fog. I bolted down several flights of stairs and out the door. Rawalt said he was working on a white-collar crime "in the vicinity." In the vicinity was as close as he was going to come to GPS coordinates. A helicopter was required for this assignment, and the helicopter was grounded by the fog. He said he just wanted to say hello.

And five years after that, I found myself in near-catastrophic frustration while I was trying to complete a book, the final part of which was planned to involve a journey in a Union Pacific coal train. Over many months, I had prepared for the event, and the railroad had encouraged me, but now the railroad was doing the Jackie Gleason. I called a couple of times a day—day after day after day—and the calls were not returned, by company people in Omaha who had earlier given me a week of invaluable orientation, including visits to the Union Pacific rail yard in Council Bluffs, Iowa, and to "the bunker," an impregnable building in Omaha where dispatchers control everything that is happening on nineteen thousand miles of track. And now, a couple of months later, I was back home calling Omaha, listening to a machine, and leaving messages. My book was dead in the water, and my wits seemed to have come to an end. A light turned on. I called Ron Rawalt. Maybe he could help. The rail yard in North Platte is the largest in the world. Rawalt said, "Fly to Denver and drive to North Platte." A day and a half later, I was having breakfast with the local secretary-treasurer of the United Transportation Union, the local chairman of the Brotherhood of Locomotive Engineers, and Rawalt. The morning after that, I was out on the Triple-Track Main, rolling for Kansas, in the cab of a Union Pacific coal train seven thousand four hundred and eighty-five feet long.

•

For most of the cover stories I worked on in the early nineteen-sixties at *Time*, other people did all or most of the reporting, and I did the writing. This ecumenical format, known as group journalism, was created by Henry Luce, whose most formative years were spent in the China Inland Mission School in Chefoo. Today his creation would be called cloud journalism, a form of utopian commune. Reports known as files came to writers and editors in New York from the magazine's bureaus around the country and the world. As a would-be wordsmith, I wanted to be the writer of every sentence in my pieces large and small, so (like most of the other writers in the "back of the book") I used the reporters' files as references and sources of quotes but did not cobble pieces together from this chunk and that chunk of other peoples' words. No pieces were signed.

I wrote a cover story on Sophia Loren.

Her feet are too big. Her nose is too long. Her teeth are
uneven. She has the neck, as one of her rivals has put it,
of "a Neapolitan giraffe." Her waist seems to begin in
the middle of her thighs, and she has big, half-bushel
hips. She runs like a fullback. Her hands are huge. Her
forehead is low. Her mouth is too large. And, mamma
mia, she is absolutely gorgeous.

But she was in Italy and I was in New York practicing mis-
sionary journalism. I never met her (I think I would remember if I had). I never met Joan Baez or Mort Sahl. I did a lot of
the reporting on a Jean Kerr cover and a bit on Barbra Streisand, who had an apartment on the Upper West Side. Week
by week, writing the short takeouts and news pieces in the
Show Business section, I got to do a percentage of the reporting as well as all of the writing, better experience than I ever
would have had in sections like Foreign News or National
Affairs. Anomalously, I was assigned to do essentially a hundred
per cent of the reporting as well as the writing not only for the
Gleason story but also for a 1963 cover story on Richard Burton.
      Now and again, across two years after I met Burton in To-
ronto, where he was opening in *Camelot*, I proposed a Burton
cover to Otto Fuerbringer. I had gone to Toronto assigned to
write about Alan Jay Lerner and Frederick Loewe, lyricist and
composer of *Camelot*, whose previous collaboration had been
My Fair Lady. The foci of that visit were Lerner and Loewe,
not Burton, so I had come to know him casually and not in a
formal way. I thought he was about as great an actor as an actor
could be. And, as it happened, I remembered his debut season
as Hamlet at the Old Vic, during which I had seen him twice
while I was a student in England. Eventually, I would write:

Then as now, opening nights petrified him. He does not
sleep at all before them. One evening in 1953 he left his

home in Hampstead to walk, he thought, aimlessly; but toward four a.m. he was crossing Waterloo Bridge, beyond which was the Old Vic, some ten miles from his home. A policeman stopped him on the bridge and wanted to know who he was. Richard explained that he was a terrified actor. On the following night, he was going to open as Hamlet, Prince of Denmark, at the Old Vic. "Oh, come now," said the bobby. "They won't know in Peckham Rye, will they? They won't know in St. John's Wood." Burton relaxed slightly and walked out the night with the bobby, making the rounds of Waterloo.

In the *Camelot* company's hotel in Toronto, Burton would retreat after dinner to his room with other actors, grips, stagehands, and whatnot. Talk would go on until three in the morning. As whatnot, I was entranced. So back in New York I proposed a cover on him, but Fuerbringer repeatedly turned me down until Burton checked into the Dorchester in London with Elizabeth Taylor and was being described as one of the two most famous people in the world. Fuerbringer called me into his office and said that what *Time* had long needed was a cover story on Richard Burton. Yes, I said, and I hope I can describe him as an actor. Responding to a query not from me but from the magazine, Burton said he would cooperate if I were the interviewer as well as the writer.

A lot of the interviewing was accomplished inside a Rolls-Royce. A Silver Cloud, it was parked each morning outside 53 Park Lane, waiting for Burton and Taylor, each of whom was married to someone else, to come down from their penthouse suite and depart for work. They were making a movie called *The V.I.P.s* at a studio close to Heathrow, and the trip each way took an hour. The director, Anthony Asquith, whose father had been Prime Minister of the United Kingdom during the First World War, liked shooting at sunrise, so the Rolls left the Dorchester as early as 5 and no later than 6 a.m. I was staying up the street in Grosvenor House, at 86 Park Lane, and for more than a week was in the car waiting when Taylor and Burton appeared.

She was never sleepy. In Burton's case, it was hard to tell. At least once, he had been in Hampstead talking with his wife, Sybil, until three or four in the morning, returning to the Dorchester in time for little more than a drink or two before descending to the Silver Cloud. Sybil told me this, and much else, on the telephone. She said he had consumed an entire bottle of cognac in the hours he was with her. Rémy Martin. I failed to ask what size. No matter what his blood-alcohol level might be, Burton the actor never missed a director's call. He claimed so at the time, and that was his reputation as well. On those mornings at 5 a.m., I surely had reason to believe him.

At the studio, he was prepared for action from the first minute, and when he was not shooting a scene, which was most of the time, he was talking to other actors, grips, stage-hands, and whatnot. He related to everybody. He talked football endlessly, and, most impressively, he listened. Drawing some-one out about Manchester United or Tottenham Hotspur, he listened with evident interest and occasional comment. He asked me about my three children in New Jersey. Three daughters! Splendid. He had only two.

Also in the studio was Maggie Smith, a young beauty still in her twenties, with her large eyes, her incisive face, her auburn hair. She was playing a small role as a quiet secretary secretly in love with her employer. When Maggie Smith was not acting, she sat reading, oblivious of the tabloid whirl around her. Take note of her, Burton said; she has more talent than anyone else in the building. After doing a scene with her, he said he had been overshadowed and outacted. Written by the playwright Terence Rattigan, the film, set at Heathrow, was about a rich man's wife running off with a lover, but Heathrow is fogged in, and her husband shows up to plead with her. Other passengers, also star-crossed, are analogously inconvenienced. Rattigan said the germ of the story came from Vivien Leigh ("Frankly, my dear, I don't give a damn"), who was married to Laurence Olivier but fell in love with another actor and was fogged in at Heathrow trying to run off with him.

Burton was even easier to interview than Woody Allen, because he interviewed himself. You just listened, and wrote down what he said. At the studio, most of that happened in Elizabeth Taylor's dressing room, which was not a cramped space. There was a couch, a coffee table, plenty of room for walking around. She feigned irritation that I was all but completely concentrating on Burton. I'm sure she understood what I was doing and did not seriously care. But she kept interrupting us. She was having fun. And so was I, for sure. In comparison with a great many of the actresses I had met in my years of writing about show business, she was not even half full of herself. She seemed curious, sophisticated, and unpretentious, and compared to people I had known in universities she seemed to have been particularly well educated. From childhood forward, she was tutored in the cafeteria at M-G-M.

One day, she interrupted us with the news that a pair of British journalists were about to arrive for a scheduled interview with her and Burton. It was all right if I wanted to stay and listen, but my own interview had to be suspended. Sure. Thanks. This would be interesting. Both were men. Both were tall and, as I remember, oddly diffident. Sitting side by side on the couch, they asked chatty questions and made occasional chatty comments. They recorded nothing and made no notes. Taylor gave them tea. The teacups rested on their knees— easy to maintain, since the writers were not writing. On the following day, their update on the world's preeminent scandal appeared on the front page of their newspaper. The piece was full of quotes—long quotes, short quotes, hyposensational

quotes. But the writers seemed to lack the mnemonic skills of
Truman Capote. At any rate, I couldn't recall hearing Taylor
or Burton say any of the skeins of words attributed to them
within quotation marks. This was seven years before Rupert
Murdoch bought *News of the World.*

When the British journalists were gone and I got back to
the broken lance I was carrying, Burton returned to his story
about 1953 at the Old Vic:

That his performance would be recorded far beyond
St. John's Wood was largely due to a critical remark made
more than midway in *Hamlet's* run. Burton's Hamlet
was something like a corrida, good one night, disap-
pointing the next. But when he had his color and gave it
the full Welsh timbre, he thrilled audiences long accus-
tomed to the tremulous Gielgud reading. He had completed about sixty performances and the box office was
beginning to slide when the house manager came to his
dressing room one evening and said, "Be especially good
tonight. The old man's out front."

"What old man?"

"He comes once a year," said the house manager.
"He stays for one act and he leaves."

"For God's sake, what old man?"

"Churchill."

As Burton spoke his first line—"A little more than
kin, and less than kind"—he was startled to hear deep
identical mutterings from the front row. Churchill continued to follow him line for line, a dramaturgical beagle,
his face a thunderhead when something had been cut.
"I tried to shake him off," Burton remembers. "I went
fast and I went slow, but he was right there." Churchill
was right there to the end, in fact, when Burton took
eighteen curtain calls and Churchill told a reporter: "It

was as exciting and virile a performance of *Hamlet* as I can remember." Years later, when *Winston Churchill— The Valiant Years* was under preparation for television, its producers asked Sir Winston who he thought should do the voice of Churchill. "Get that boy from the Old Vic," said the old man.

They got that boy from the Old Vic.

Frame of Reference

In 2000, Abe Crystal, an undergraduate from Columbia, South Carolina, was enrolled in the writing class I teach at Princeton, and one of his assignments was to compose a profile of another student, whose name was Grainger David. This Grainger happened to be the undergraduate president of F. Scott Fitzgerald's University Cottage Club and was as smoothly verbal and self-possessed as any of Fitzgerald's characters, including Amory Blaine, of *This Side of Paradise*. In the profile, Abe Crystal mentioned, without amplification, that Grainger David had "sprezzatura."

Sprezzatura? Of course in this advanced age of the handheld vocabulary, everyone on earth knows what sprezzatura means, but in 2000 I had no idea, and I reached for an Italian dictionary. Nothing. I looked in another Italian dictionary. Nothing. I looked in Web II—Webster's unabridged New International Dictionary, Second Edition. Niente. I picked up the phone and called my daughter Martha, who has lived in Italy and co-translated John Paul II's *Crossing the Threshold of Hope* into English from the Vatican's Italian.

Her credentials notwithstanding, Martha was no help.

I tried my daughter Sarah, a professor of art and architectural history at Emory, whose specialty is Baroque Rome. Her answering machine was as helpful as Martha.

That evening, I happened to attend a crowded reception at the New York Public Library with my daughter Jenny, the other translator of the Pope's book, and her husband, Luca Passaleva, who was born, raised, and educated in Florence. "Hey, Luc. What is the meaning of 'sprezzatura'?"

Luca: "I don't know. Ask Jenny."

Jenny: "I don't know, but that couple over there might know. He's in the Italian consulate."

Consul: "Ask my wife. She is literary, I am not."

Signora: "I'm very sorry. I have no idea."

Back in Princeton next day, I had a scheduled story conference with Abe Crystal, his profile of Grainger David on the desk in front of us. With my index finger touching "sprezzatura," I said, "Abe, what the hell is this?"

Abe said he had picked up the word in Castiglione's *The Courtier*, 1528. "It means effortless grace, all easy, doing something cool without apparent effort."

Soon after he left, I called Sarah again, and she picked up. She said Abe had it right but the word "nonchalance" should be added to his definition. She said that Raphael carried the ideal of sprezzatura into painting. "He painted his friend Baldassare Castiglione as the ideal courtier, the embodiment of sprezzatura. It's now in the Louvre."

•

Robert Bingham, my editor at *The New Yorker* for sixteen years, had a fluorescent, not to mention distinguished, mustache. In some piece or other, early on, I said of a person I was writing about that he had a "sincere" mustache. This brought Bingham, manuscript in hand, out of his office and down the hall to mine, as I had hoped it would. A sincere mustache, Mr. McPhee, a sincere mustache? What does that mean? Was I implying that it is possible to have an insincere mustache?

I said I could not imagine anything said more plainly.

The mustache made it into the magazine and caused me to feel self-established as *The New Yorker*'s nonfiction mustache specialist. Across time, someone came along who had "a no-nonsense-mustache," and a Great Lakes ship captain who had "a gyroscopic mustache," and a North Woodsman who had "a timber-cruiser's guileless mustache." A family practitioner in Maine had "an analgesic mustache," another doctor "a soothing mustache," and another a mustache that "seems medical, in that it spreads flat beyond the corners of his mouth and suggests no prognosis, positive or negative."

Writing has to be fun at least once in a pale blue moon.

Dodge had a great deal more hair on his upper lip than elsewhere on his head. With his grand odobene mustache he had everything but the tusks. . . . His words filtered softly through the Guinness book mustache. It was really a sight to see, like a barrel on his lip.

Inevitably, all this led to Andrew Lawson. Andrew Lawson? The great Scottish-born Andrew Lawson, structural geologist, University of California, Berkeley, who named—perhaps eponymously—the San Andreas Fault. Andrew Lawson was lowered in a bucket into a caisson in San Francisco Bay in order to decide if the south pier of the Golden Gate Bridge could be constructed where it is.

With his pure-white hair, his large frame, his tetragrammatonic mustache, Lawson personified Higher Authority.

Querying letters poured into the *New Yorker* office like water over the sides of a caisson. With utmost generosity, the

writer Charles McGrath, then a young *New Yorker* editor, vol-
untarily answered them.

•

A tetragrammatonic anything and a term that seems to have
stalled in the Italian Renaissance are points of reference that
might just irritate rather than illuminate some readers. Make
that most readers. The perpetrator is the writer. Mea culpa.
Meanwhile, though, in a contrary way, we have come upon a
topic of first importance in the making of a piece of writing: its
frame of reference, the things and people you choose to allude
to in order to advance its comprehensibility. Mention Beyoncé
and everyone knows who she is. Mention Veronica Lake and
you might as well be in the Quetico-Superior. A discussion
like this demands an added lamination: When was it written?
It was written in the second decade of the twenty-first century.
Obviously, if you mention New York, you can count on most
readers to know what that is and where. Mention Vernal Corners and you can't. It's upstate. What would you do with
Scarsdale? Do you need to say where it is? Step van, Stanley
Steamer, black-and-white unit, gooseneck trailer. If you know
what a gooseneck trailer is, raise your hand.

One hand rises among thirty-two.

"Where are you from, Stacey?"

"Idaho."

To sense the composite nature of frames of reference, think
of their incidental aftermath, think of some old ones as they
have moved through time, eventually forming distinct strata
in history. At the University of Cambridge, academic supervisors
in English literature would hand you a photocopy of an un-
identified swatch of prose or poetry and ask you to say in what
decade of what century it was written. This custom is called
dating and is not as difficult as you might imagine. A useful

comparison is to the science of geochronology, which I once
tried to explain with this description:

> Imagine an E. L. Doctorow novel in which Alfred Ten-
> nyson, William Tweed, Abner Doubleday, Jim Bridger,
> and Martha Jane Canary sit down to a dinner cooked
> by Rutherford B. Hayes. Geologists would call that a
> fossil assemblage. And, without further assistance from
> Doctorow, a geologist could quickly decide—as could
> anyone else—that the dinner must have occurred in the
> middle eighteen-seventies, because Canary was eighteen
> when the decade began, Tweed became extinct in 1878,
> and the biographies of the others do not argue with these
> limits.

Fossils were the isotopes of their time, and that is how, in
the nineteenth century, the science developed the story it was
telling. All this is only to show how frames of reference operate,
how quickly they evolve from currency to obsolescence. The
last thing I would ever suggest to young writers is that they
consciously try to write for the ages. Oh, yik, disgusting. Nobody
should ever be trying that. We should just be hoping that our
pieces aren't obsolete before the editor sees them. If you look
for allusions and images that have some durability, your choices
will stabilize your piece of writing. Don't assume that everyone
on earth has seen every movie you have seen. In the archives
of ersatz references, that one is among the fattest folders.
"This recalled the climb-out scene in *Deliverance*." "That
was like the ending of *Bird Man of Alcatraz*."

Here is a lively group pieced together by Sarah Boxer,
writing in 2010 in *The New York Review of Books* about the
artists Hedda Sterne and Saul Steinberg, who "knew all
the *New Yorker* people, the writers and cartoonists and movie

people—Charlie Addams, Cobean, William Steig, Peter Arno, Ian Frazier, Dwight Macdonald, Harold Rosenberg, E. B. White, Katharine White—and they all came to dinner." That's a fossil assemblage with a virus in it. Ian Frazier, in Hudson, Ohio, in the era of those dinners, was nine years old and younger.

Frames of reference are like the constellation of lights, some of them blinking, on an airliner descending toward an airport at night. You see the lights. They imply a structure you can't see. Inside that frame of reference—those descending lights— is a big airplane with its flaps down expecting a runway.

•

You will never land smoothly on borrowed vividness. If you say someone looks like Tom Cruise—and you let it go at that— you are asking Tom Cruise to do your writing for you. Your description will fail when your reader doesn't know who Tom Cruise is.

Who is Tom Ripley?

Dwight Garner in *The New York Times*, 2010: "Castelli was a hard man to know. He had thousands of friends but few intimates. There was something elusive, shape-shifting, almost Tom Ripley–like about him."

More scattered examples from not-very-bygone years:

John Leonard, *The New York Times Book Review*, 2005, reviewing the Library of America's collection of James Agee: "Who knows what marriage was, maybe musical electric chairs. Add it all up, tossing in macho rubbish about tomcatting and romantic beeswax about the agony of artistic creation, and what you don't get is a grown-up. You get Rufus in Knoxville."

Janet Maslin, *The New York Times*, 2008, reviewing *The Memoirs of a Beautiful Boy*, by Robert Leleux: "Despite many obstacles, not least of them the danger of sounding like a would-be Augusten Burroughs, he has made her the center-piece of a frantically giddy coming-of-age story."

Maureen Dowd, *The New York Times*, 2008, on President emeritus William Jefferson Clinton: "Bill continues to howl at the moon. . . . He's starting to make King Lear look like Ryan Seacrest."

Joel Achenbach, in his wonderful book *Captured by Aliens* (1999), page 391: "There's a nebula in space that looks like Abe Vigoda."

Joel, as a college senior, was in my writing class in 1982. I keep trying. Also in *Captured by Aliens*, he produces this description of a professor at Tufts University: "He looks a bit like Gene Wilder, and has some of the same manic energy." Gene Wilder? Search me. But nota bene: when Joel says "the same manic energy," he is paying back much of the vividness he borrowed.

Enter Robert Wright, who was in the class four years earlier and has become an author who will take on subjects few would dare to confront, such as *The Evolution of God* in five hundred and seventy-six pages (2009). His first book (1988) was called *Three Scientists and Their Gods*. Chapter 19 begins this way: "The fact that Kenneth Boulding is a Quaker does not mean that he looks like the Quaker on the cartons of Quaker Oats."

Bob does not seem interested in the future of that allusion, but he does go on to say,

As it turns out, there is a certain resemblance. Both men have shoulder-length, snow-white hair, blue eyes, and ruddy cheeks, and both have fundamentally sunny dispositions, smiling much or all of the time, respectively. There are differences, to be sure. Boulding's hair is not as cottony as the Oats Quaker's, and it falls less down and more back, skirting the tops of his ears along the way. And Boulding's face is not soft and generic. His nose is jutting, and his eyes are deeply set and profoundly knowing.

Borrowed vividness may never have been so amply repaid. Trevor Corson, in *The Zen of Fish*, 2007: "Salmon smell their way back to their birthplace. . . . As they head upriver they also undergo astonishing anatomical changes, not unlike Dr. David Banner's transforming into the Incredible Hulk."

Bruce Handy, *The New York Times Book Review*, 2005, on Jonathan Harr's *The Lost Painting*: "Today, the dirty feet of Caravaggio's models don't distract us from his formal beauty—gosh, we're inured to Nan Goldin. . . . It is one of the artist's most intimate religious paintings—a tight medium shot in Hollywood terms, the action filling the frame with a choreographed immediacy Michael Bay must admire if he's ever seen it."

Michael Pollan, *The New York Times Magazine*, 2002: "Watching a steer force-marched up the ramp to the kill-floor door, as I have done, I need to remind myself that this is not Sean Penn in *Dead Man Walking*, that in a bovine brain the concept of nonexistence is blissfully absent."

Mark Singer, in *Somewhere in America*, 2004, paying off with so much interest that he has no debt: "Keys lacks the aura and demeanor of a politician. He's sixty years old, pink-faced and freckled, with red hair that's completing the transition to white. His drooping mustache, wire-rimmed glasses, plaid shirts, and blue jeans give him the overall look of a lean Wilford Brimley."

Who Wilford Brimley? Who cares?

Ian Frazier, in *The New Yorker*, in 2014, attempting unsuccessfully to stay out of debtor's prison: "Along with playing conga drums, she throws pots and is pursuing her second M.A., in experimental psychology with a focus on marine biology. She looks enough like the late Bea Arthur, the star of the nineteen-seventies sitcom *Maude*, that it would be negligent not to say so."

•

Frames of reference are grossly abused by writers and broad-casters of the punch-line school. We're approaching the third decade of the twenty-first century and someone on Fox refers coyly to "a band called the Beatles and another called the Rolling Stones." Y2kute. And NPR is reviewing the life of *The Washington Post*'s Ben Bradlee: "He became close to a Georgetown neighbor—a young senator named John F. Kennedy." Doesn't that give you a shiver in the bones? Pure pall-esthesia. Ta-da!

The columnist Frank Bruni, writing in *The New York Times* in 2014, said, "If you . . . want to feel much, much older, teach a college course. I'm doing that now . . . and hardly a class goes by when I don't make an allusion that prompts my students to stare at me as if I just dropped in from the Paleozoic era. . . . I once brought up Vanessa Redgrave. Blank stares. Greta Garbo. Ditto. We were a few minutes into a discussion of an essay that repeatedly invoked Proust's madeleine when I realized that almost none of the students understood what the made-leine signified or, for that matter, who this Proust fellow was."

As it happened, Frank Bruni was at Princeton teaching in the same program I teach in—same classroom, same semester, different course, different day—and if I had felt "much, much older" I would have been back in the Archean Eon. Frank wrote that he was wondering if all of us are losing what he felicitously called our "collective vocabulary." He asked, "Are common points of reference dwindling? Has the personal niche supplanted the public square?"

My answer would be that the collective vocabulary and

common points of reference are not only dwindling now but have been for centuries. The dwindling may have become speedier, but it is an old and continuous condition. I am forever testing my students to see what works and does not work in pieces of varying vintage.

"Y2K—what does that mean?"

No one knew before the late nineties, and how long will the term last if it isn't gone already?

Y2K QE2 P-38 B-29 Enola Gay NFL NBA CBS NBC Fox? Do you watch comets?

A couple of weeks before that spring semester began, I had been in Massachusetts collecting impressions for this project by testing the frame of reference in "Elicitation," which was soon to run in *The New Yorker*. Why Massachusetts? Because that's where Brookline High School is and where Mary Burchenal's senior English classes meet, and where Isobel McPhee, daughter of my daughter Laura, was one of her students. The article's frame of reference consisted of about five dozen items running along the edges of seven thousand words.

"I would like to try that list on you. Raise your hand if you recognize these names and places: Woody Allen."

Nineteen hands went up. Everybody present in the class that day was aware of Woody Allen. As we went through my list, nineteen hands went up also for Muhammad Ali, *Time* magazine, Hallmark cards, Denver, Mexico, Princeton University, Winston Churchill, *Hamlet*, and Toronto. So those perfect scores reached around about fifteen per cent of the frame.

Sarah Palin, Omaha, Barbra Streisand, Rolls-Royce—18.

Paul Newman—17.

Heathrow—16.

Fort Knox—15.

Elizabeth Taylor, *My Fair Lady*—11.

Cassius Clay—8.

Waterloo Bridge, Maggie Smith—6.

Norman Rockwell, Truman Capote, Joan Baez—5.
Rupert Murdoch—3.
Hampstead, Mickey Rooney—2.
Richard Burton, Laurence Olivier, Vivien Leigh—1.
"In England, would you know what a bobby is?"—1.
Calabria, St. John's Wood, Peckham Rye, Churchill Downs, the Old Vic, *News of the World*, Jackie Gleason, David Brower, Ralph Nelson, David Susskind, Jack Dempsey, Stephen Harper, Thomas P. F. Hoving, George Plimpton, J. Anthony Lukas, Bob Woodward, Norman Maclean, Henry Luce, Sophia Loren, Mort Sahl, Jean Kerr, James Boswell, Samuel Johnson—0.

•

In 1970, I went to Wimbledon on an assignment from *Playboy*. The idea was to spend the whole of the championships fortnight there and then write a montage of impressions, not only of the players but also of the place. The eventual piece was quite long but its freestanding parts were short, like this one:

Hoad on Court 5, weathered and leonine, has come from Spain, where he lives on his tennis ranch in the plains of Andalusia. Technically, he is an old hero trying a comeback but, win or lose, with this crowd it is enough of a comeback that Hoad is here. There is tempestuous majesty in him, and people have congregated seven deep around his court just to feel the atmosphere there and to see him again. Hoad serves explosively, and the ball hits the fence behind his opponent without first intersecting the ground. His precision is off. The dead always rise slowly.

And so on to the end of Hoad, which was imminent. Meanwhile:

Smith, in a remote part of the grounds, is slowly extin-
guishing Jaime Fillol. . . . Laver is so far ahead that the
match has long since become an exhibition.

The grounds were often more interesting than the matches,
the All England Lawn Tennis and Croquet Club being such
an index fossil from the nineteenth century.

In the Players' Tea Room, the players sit on pale-blue
wicker chairs at pale-blue wicker tables eating strawberries in Devonshire cream.

The editor of the piece was the affable Arthur Kretchmer,
who was soon to become *Playboy*'s editorial director, a position
he would hold for thirty years. My conferences with him, always
on the telephone, were light and without speed bumps as we
made our way through the strawberries, the extinguishings, and
the resurrections, until we came to the Members' Enclosure.

In the Members' Enclosure, on the Members' Lawn,
members and their guests are sitting under white
parasols, consuming best-end-of-lamb salad and strawberries in Devonshire cream. Around them are pools of
goldfish. The goldfish are rented from Harrods. The
members are rented from the uppermost upper middle
class. Wimbledon is the annual convention of this stratum of English society, starboard out, starboard home.

Arthur Kretchmer said, "What does that mean?"
Assuming a tone of faintest surprise, I explained that when
English people went out to India during the Raj, they went in
unairconditioned ships. The most expensive staterooms were
on the port side, away from the debilitating sun. When they
sailed westward home, the most expensive staterooms were

on the starboard side, for the same reason. And that is the actual or apocryphal but nonetheless commonplace etymology of the word "posh." Those people in the All England Members' Enclosure were one below Ascot: starboard out, starboard home.

I didn't have a stopwatch with which to time the length of the silence on the other end of the line. I do remember what Kretchmer eventually said. He said, "Maybe one reader in ten thousand would get that."

I said, "Look: you have bought thirteen thousand words about Wimbledon with no other complaint. I beg you to keep it as it is for that one reader."

He said, "Sold!"

Checkpoints

Sara Lippincott, who now lives in Pasadena, having retired as an editor at *The New Yorker* in the early nineteen-nineties, worked in the magazine's fact-checking department from 1966 until 1982. She had a passion for science, and when pieces of writing about science came into the magazine they were generally copied to her desk. In 1973, a long piece of mine called "The Curve of Binding Energy" received her full-time attention for three or four weeks and needed every minute of it. Explaining her work to an audience at a journalism school, Sara once said, "Each word in the piece that has even a shred of fact clinging to it is scrutinized, and, if passed, given the checker's imprimatur, which consists of a tiny pencil tick." From that sixty-thousand-word piece of mine—which was about weapons-grade nuclear material in private industry and what terrorists might or might not do with it—one paragraph in particular stands out in memory for the degree of difficulty it presented to her and the effort she made to keep it or kill it.

It was a story told to me by John A. Wheeler, who, during the Second World War, had been the leading physicist in residence at the Hanford Engineer Works, on the Columbia River in south-central Washington, where he attended the startup and plutonium production of the first large-scale nuclear reactor in the world. In 1939, with the Danish physicist Niels Bohr, Wheeler had identified the atomic nuclei most prone to fission and the consequent release of binding energy. In 1943–44, as the first reactor was being designed for Hanford, Wheeler had urged that its fundamental cross-section be expanded from a circle to a square, so that five hundred extra fuel rods could be inserted, if necessary, into the graphite matrix of the reactor— a colossally expensive alteration made because Wheeler had come to suspect that something like xenon poisoning might affect the reaction. It did, and the increased neutron flux from the additional fuel rods took care of the problem. In Professor Wheeler's office at Princeton University in 1973, I had scribbled notes for about an hour when he said, as a kind of afterthought, that an odd thing happened at Hanford in the winter of 1944–45, or, perhaps, did not happen. He had not observed it himself. He had never seen it mentioned in print. Hanford was a vast, spread-out place in the bunchgrass country, full of rumors, secrecy, and apocryphal stories. If I were to use this story, I would have to authenticate it on my own because he had no idea if it was true. He said he had heard that a Japanese incendiary balloon—one of the weapon balloons that were released in Japan and carried by the jet stream across the Pacific Ocean—had landed on the reactor that was making the plutonium that destroyed Nagasaki, and had shut the reactor down.

The Japanese called the balloons *fūsen bakudan*. Thirty-three feet in diameter, they were made of paper and were equipped with incendiary devices or high explosives. In less than a year, nine thousand were launched from a beach on Honshu. They killed six people in Oregon, five of them children, and they started forest fires, and they landed from Alaska to Mexico and as far east as Farmington, Michigan, a suburb of Detroit. Completing the original manuscript of "The Curve of Binding Energy," which was otherwise not about Hanford, I wrote half a dozen sentences on the balloon that shut down the reactor, and I turned the piece in. If Wheeler's story was true, it would make it into print. If unverifiable, it would be deleted. I hoped it was true. The rest was up to Sara.

Her telephone calls ricocheted all over the United States: from Brookhaven to Bethesda, from La Jolla to Los Alamos, not to mention Hanford and various targets in the District of Columbia. Interspersed with everything else she had to do in order to arrive—one word at a time—at those countless ticks, she went on making calls about the incendiary balloon for days on end. At last came an apparent breakthrough. Someone told her that he could not authenticate the story, but he knew absolutely who could.

"Oh, yes? Who?"

"John Wheeler."

I told Sara to abandon the anecdote. The tale was almost surely someone's invention; we should just delete it; she had done enough. She went on making phone calls.

If Sara was looking for information in the dark, the darkness was the long shadow of the wartime secrecy, when forty-five thousand people, from construction workers to theoreticians, lived in Hanford, Pasco, Kennewick, and, especially, Richland, a village of two hundred that the Army bought in 1943 and soon enhanced with more than four thousand houses. The large population notwithstanding, Hanford Engineer Works, of the Manhattan Project, was so secret that the Joint Chiefs of Staff did not know about it. Harry Truman learned of it only after the death of Franklin Roosevelt, in April, 1945. People at Hanford lived among posters that said "Don't Be Caught With Your Mouth Open." They set their urine in bottles on their doorsteps at night so it could be tested for contained plutonium. The people of Richland made babies at a higher rate than any other place in the nation. There was little else to make except plutonium. To put an ear to the ground, so to speak, and listen for spies, a resident F.B.I. agent went to brothels in Pasco and Kennewick, taking with him his beautiful wife. She sat in the car while he did his counterespionage inside. To profile people who might be easy targets for spies, F.B.I. agents went from house to house trying to learn who the heavier drinkers were and who was climbing into what neighbor's bed. Hanford Engineer Works had its own justices of the peace, its own jail. Taverns were erected for the nighttime bibulation of construction workers, whose tendency to brawl was so intense that Wheeler later recalled "those beer joints with windows close to ground level so that tear gas could be squirted in."

Key personnel were known by false names. Enrico Fermi was Mr. Farmer. Eugene Wigner was Mr. Winger. Arthur Compton was Mr. Comas. People referred to Wheeler as Johnny the Genie. Radiation exposure was called "shine," and the word for radiation itself was "activity." One technician who slipped up and used the "R" word was called to an office and chewed. With extremely few exceptions, the personnel had no idea what they were doing, but they did what they were told ("We all washed our hands so many times a day I thought I was Lady Macbeth"). The Manhattan Project, at Hanford as elsewhere, required the "'immediate high amputation' of any human limb with a cut contaminated by plutonium." There could have been a safety billboard: 29 DAYS WITHOUT A HUMERUS LOST. There were black-widow spiders in people's houses. One woman called the government hospital and asked what she should do if a black widow bit her three-year-old daughter. Hospital: "If she goes into convulsions, bring her in. . . ." On and off the site, rumors were ceaseless about Hanford's contribution to the war effort: variously, it was a P.O.W. camp, a processor of solid rocket fuel, a biological kitchen preparing things for germ warfare, a nylon production line (DuPont was the prime industrial contractor). Asked what was really going on, the Army's knowledgeable liaison, Captain Frank Valente, said, "We are dehydrating the Columbia River for shipment overseas."

And now, in late 1973 at *The New Yorker,* the moment was rapidly approaching when "The Curve of Binding Energy" would go to press and alterations would no longer be possible. Once again I thanked Sara and told her to remove the story of the Japanese balloon. O.K., she said, but maybe if she found a free moment that final afternoon she would make another call or two. Or three. And she did, and she turned up someone in Delaware who told her that he could not authenticate the story, but he knew absolutely who could.

Oh? Who would that be? John Wheeler?

The site manager, B Reactor. He would surely have known if an incendiary balloon had lit up his building.

Where is he now?

Retired in Florida.

Sara looked up his telephone number. The checking department in those days was equipped floor-to-ceiling with telephone books. She called. He was not home. He had gone shopping.

Where?

The mall.

Sara called the police. She told them the situation, asked for help, and gave them her telephone number.

Minutes went by but not hours. The piece had not yet gone to press when the site manager called. He was in a telephone booth, the ancestral cell. Sara explained her purpose and read to him a passage that ended as follows:

The fire balloons were so successful, in fact, that papers were asked not to print news of them, because the United States did not want to encourage the Japanese to release more. The balloon that reached Hanford crossed not only the Pacific but also the Olympic Mountains and the

alpine glaciers of the Cascade Range. It now landed
on the building containing the reactor that was producing the Nagasaki plutonium, and shut the reactor down.

The manager said to Sara, "How did you know that?"
He went on to say that the balloon had not actually landed
on the building but on a high-tension line carrying power to
the reactor. Striking the line, the balloon burst into flames.
There was just enough time to make the fix.

•

Derek Jeter, Cal Ripken Jr., and Pee Wee Reese made occasional errors, and so does *The New Yorker*. Rarest of all is a
fact that was not erroneous in the original manuscript but
became an error in the checking process. When this happens,
it can fairly be called an event, like the day the soap sank. This
has happened to me only once—and long ago. If blame is to
be assigned, heaven forbid, I am not the assignee, and neither
is Sara, who checked the piece. Called "Basin and Range," it
was the first in the series of long pieces on geology that appeared from time to time across a dozen years. It had extensive introductory passages on themes like plate tectonics and
geologic time. In the original manuscript, one paragraph said:

It is the plates that move. They all move. They move in
varying directions and at different speeds. The Adriatic
Plate is moving north. The African Plate once came up
behind it and drove it into Europe—drove Italy like a
nail into Europe—and thus created the Alps.

C Issue, B Issue, A Issue, the schedule drifted, as ever,
toward the brink of time, the final and irreversible closing. In
one's head as in the surrounding building, things speed up in
the ultimate hours and can become, to say the least, frenetic.

Joshua Hersh, a modern fact-checker who was characteristically calmer than marble, referred to this zone of time as "the last-minute heebie-jeebies." As "Basin and Range" came within fifteen minutes of closing, so many rocks were flying around in my head that I would have believed Sara if she had told me that limestone is the pit of a fruit. At one minute to zero, she came to tell me that I was wrong about the Adriatic Plate, that it is not moving north but southwest.

Desperately, I said, "Who told you that?"

She said, "Eldridge Moores."

World-class plate theorist, author of innumerable scientific papers on the ophiolitic sequence as the signature of global tectonics, president-to-be of the Geological Society of America, Eldridge Moores was the generous and quixotic geologist who had undertaken to teach me, on field trip after field trip, the geologic history of, among other places, California, Arizona, Greece, and Cyprus. My head spinning, I said to Sara, "If Eldridge Moores says the Adriatic Plate is moving southwest, it's moving southwest. Please change the sentence."

In the new *New Yorker* on the following Monday, the Adriatic Plate was on its way to Morocco. Leafing through the magazine in an idle moment that week, I called Eldridge and found him in his office at the University of California, Davis. I said, "Eldridge, if the Adriatic Plate is moving southwest, what are the Alps doing there?"

He said, "The Adriatic Plate?"

I said, "The Adriatic Plate."

I believe I actually heard him slap his forehead. "Oh, no!" he said. "Not the Adriatic Plate! The Aegean Plate. The Aegean Plate is moving southwest."

•

The worst checking error is calling people dead who are not dead. In the words of Joshua Hersh, "It really annoys them."

Sara remembers a reader in a nursing home who read in *The New Yorker* that he was "the late" reader in the nursing home. He wrote demanding a correction. *The New Yorker*, in its next issue, of course complied, inadvertently doubling the error, because the reader died over the weekend while the magazine was being printed.

Any error is everlasting. As Sara told the journalism students, once an error gets into print it "will live on and on in libraries carefully catalogued, scrupulously indexed . . . silicon-chipped, deceiving researcher after researcher down through the ages, all of whom will make new errors on the strength of the original errors, and so on and on into an exponential explosion of errata." With drawn sword, the fact-checker stands at the near end of this bridge. It is, in part, why the job exists and why, in Sara's words, a publication will believe in "turning a pack of professional skeptics loose on its own galley proofs." Newspapers do not have discrete fact-checking departments, but many magazines do. When I first worked at *Time*—in the year 1957, during the reign of Eadwig the All-Fair—*Time*'s writers were men and the researcher/fact-checkers were women. They were expert. When I freelanced a piece to *The Atlantic*, I asked who would do the fact-checking and was told, "That's up to you." *The Atlantic* had a nil budget for fact-checking. A little later, when I sold a piece to *National Geographic* it seemed to have more fact-checkers than there are Indians in the Amazon. *Holiday* and *The Saturday Evening Post* were only a little less assiduous. While *The New Yorker*'s fact-checking department had achieved early fame in its field, many other magazines have been just as committed and careful. Twenty-eight years after that first *Atlantic* piece, I sold *The Atlantic* a second one, and this time experienced a checking process equivalent to *The New Yorker*'s.

Book publishers prefer to regard fact-checking as the responsibility of authors, which, contractually, comes down to a simple matter of who doesn't pay for what. If material that has appeared in a fact-checked magazine reappears in a book, the author is not the only beneficiary of the checker's work. The book publisher has won a free ticket to factual respectability. Publishers who, for early-marketing purposes, set a text in stone before a magazine's checking department has been through it get what they deserve. An almost foolproof backup screen to the magazine-to-book progression is the magazine's vigilant readership. After an error gets into *The New Yorker*, heat-seeking missiles rise off the earth and home in on the author, the fact-checker, the editor, and even the shade of the founder. As the checking department summarizes it, "no mistakes go unnoticed by readers." In the waning days of 2005, Rebecca Curtis's fine short story "Twenty Grand" appeared in *The New Yorker*. Its characters, in 1979, go into a McDonald's for Chicken McNuggets. McNuggets appeared in *The New Yorker*'s Christmas mail. McDonald's had introduced them nationwide in 1983.

On the scattered occasions when such a message has come to me, I have written to the reader a note of thanks (unless the letter is somewhere on the continuum between mean-spirited and nasty, which is rarely the case). "You're right!" I say. "And I am very grateful to you, because that mistake will not be present when the piece appears in book form." If, in the reader's letter, there has been just a tonal hint of a smirk, I cannot help adding, "If a lynx-eyed reader like you has gone through those thousands of words and has found only one mistake, I am quite relieved."

•

If there is one collection of people even more likely than *New Yorker* readers to notice mistakes of any ilk or origin, it is the Swiss. Around the first of October, 1983, Richard Sacks, a fact-checking veteran with oak-leaf clusters, put on his headphones and dialed Zurich. In weeks that followed, he also called Bern, Brig, Lausanne, Geneva, Salgesch, Sion, Sierre, and other communities, many of them in the Canton de Vaud, principal home of the Swiss Army's Tenth Mountain Division, which had given me a woolly hat and allowed me to walk around in the Bernese Oberland and the Pennine Alps with the Section de Renseignements of the Eighth Battalion, Fifth Regiment. Eventually, I wrote:

> With notebooks and pencils, the patrols of the Section de Renseignements go from place to place exploring, asking questions, collecting particulars, scribbling information, characterizing and describing people and scenes, doing reconnaissance of various terrains, doing surveillance of present activity, and tracking events of the recent past. Afterward, they trudge back and, under pressure of time, compress, arrange, and present what they have heard and seen. All of that is incorporated into the substance of the word "renseignements." I have limitless empathy for the Section de Renseignements.

No problem there. All Richard had to do was ask, phrase by phrase, if the patrols did those things. If he had to ask in French, he also asked for someone who could speak English, the better to tick the phrases. There were, however, extended dimensions of the situation.

> Generally speaking, it can be said that discipline is nearly perfect in the Swiss Army, and that discipline is perhaps a little less than perfect if the soldiers are thinking in French, and, finally, that within any French-speaking battalion perfection tends to dilapidate in the Section de Renseignements.

How would you put that in a call to an official in the Département Militaire? I had made very formal application to attend
a so-called refresher course (a *cours de répétition*) with units
of the national militia, and had included only one stipulation:
that I spend at least fifty per cent of my time not in the company of officers. Evidently, the Département Militaire had no
difficulty deciding where to place me.

According to majors and manuals, Renseignements is
an activity that calls for a special style of mind, constantly
seeking intelligence and finding it even if it is not there,
for in peacetime exercises what is required above all else
is imagination. The effect of the Section de Renseignements is, in one major's words, "to make it live."

That is to say, people in Renseignements need a fact-
checker.

The patrols of Renseignements walk in the unoccupied
territory between the battalion and the enemy. They
circle high behind enemy lines. Since the mountains
are real and the enemy is not, there tends to be a certain diminution of energy during a refresher course—
particularly on the part of those who go out on patrol,
in contrast to those who stay in the command post and
think up things for the patrols to do. Essentially, the
people in the command posts are editors, trying to make
sense of the information presented by the patrols, and
by and large the patrols are collections of miscellaneous
freelancing loners, who lack enthusiasm for the military
enterprise, have various levels of antipathy to figures of
authority, and, in a phrase employed by themselves and
their officers alike, are "the black sheep of the army."

I would admire the Swiss forever for having the wit to assign me to Renseignements—a legerdemain of public relations unheard of in my country. Our patrol was led by a young viticulteur named Luc Massy, whose love of Switzerland was in inverse proportion to his love for the army. He carried on patrol his assault rifle, his tire-bouchon, and his six-centilitre verre de cave. The several wines concealed in his pack bulged like a cord of mortar shells. In an alpine meadow, the patrol sits down in a circle.

Massy fills the glass, holds it up to his eye.

"*Santé*," he says, with a nod to the rest of us, and— thoughtfully, unhurriedly—drinks it himself. Because I happen to be sitting beside him on his left, he says, "John, you are not very well placed. In my town, we drink counterclockwise." After finishing the glass, he fills it again and hands it to his right—to Jean Reidenbach. The background music is a dissonance of cattle bells. We count nineteen Brown Swiss in the meadow just below us, and they sound like the Salvation Army. A narrow red train appears far below. Coming out of a tunnel it crosses a bridge, whistling—three cars in all, the Furka-Oberalp.

In his weeks on the telephone with Switzerland, Richard Sacks had a great deal more to do than retrace the steps of one patrol from alp to alp, or call an off-limits restaurant in Birgisch where Corporal Massy stirred fondue with the antenna of a walkie-talkie. There remained that other half of the equation, the officers: the major who managed the Hotel zum Storchen, in Zurich; the colonel who was also president of Credit Suisse; the major who was general manager of the Bankverein; the colonel who was president of the Bankgesellschaft; the colonel who was chairman of Hoffmann–La Roche; the major who was chairman of Ciba-Geigy; the major who imported lobsters from Maine and had been caught entering Sweden with bundles of cash taped to his legs. Richard could not get a hard check on that last one, and we left it out of the piece. Captain François Rumpf was my official shepherd and initial contact. A letter from the Département Militaire instructed me after arriving in Switzerland to meet him on a precise day and hour in the Second Class Buffet in the railway station of Lausanne. I was there, on the Swiss dot. Rumpf was adjutant to Adrien Tschumy, the tall, contemplative Divisionnaire—two stars and a full-time professional. He reported to Enrico Franchini, of Canton Ticino, Commandant de Corps.

He had a kindly face that was somewhat wrinkled and drawn. There were three stars on his cap, and down the sides of his legs ran the broad black stripes of the general staff, disappearing into low black boots. Sometimes described as "mysterious" and "not well known outside Ticino," he was one of the seven supreme commanders of the Swiss Army.

I had worked through the final draft of the manuscript during a month at an academic retreat in northern Italy, where I had little else to do but show up for cocktails at five in the evening. I have never turned in to *The New Yorker* a more combed-over piece than that one. Its length was around forty thousand words. As Richard went through them a tick at a time—starting on the telephone in the early morning and staying on the telephone until the end of the Swiss day—he found, as he always did, errors resulting from words misheard, errors of assumption and supposition, errors of misinformation from flawed books or living sources, items misinterpreted or misunderstood. To turn up that many errors in so long a piece was routine in his work, and scarcely a surprise to me. I both expected it and depended on it in the way that I have relied on the colleagueship of professional fact-checking across the years. In the making of a long piece of factual writing, errors will occur, and in ways invisible to the writer. Was the Morgenstern really an eight-foot cudgel with a sixteen-spike pineapple head? Is the Schwarzbergalp above the Mattmarksee? Would you get to the Nussbaum bridge via Gouchheit, Krizacher, and Vogelture? Would the villages be in that order? Are there two "h"s in Gouchheit? How many "n"s in Othmar Hermann Ammann? How long would it take an entire company to go up the Bettmeralp téléphérique? How many soldiers could sleep in the Schwarzenbach barn? Was that all right with Schwarzenbach? What is the correct spelling of Schweizerische Bankgesellschaft? Of Schweizerische Kreditanstalt? Of Schweizerischer Bankverein? Who wrote the cuckoo-clock speech in Graham Greene's *The Third Man*? Did Louis Chevrolet, of Canton de Neuchâtel, really put the map of Switzerland on the grilles of his American cars? Richard called Warren, Michigan.

Richard to me, as he remembers it: "Chevy says no. Chevy denies it."

Me: "Not everything that Chevy says is right." The Musée des Suisses à l'Étranger, near Geneva, says that a map is what Chevrolet had in mind, that his emblem "*n'est pas sans rappeler, de façon stylisée, le pays d'origine du constructeur.*"

In *The Third Man*, in the immortal Ferris-wheel scene high above postwar Vienna, Orson Welles as Harry Lime implies that he has been selling diluted penicillin to Viennese hospitals but asks his lifelong friend Joseph Cotten if one of those little moving dots down there (one of those human beings) could really matter in the long scheme of things. On the ground, he adds:

> In Italy for thirty years under the Borgias, they had warfare, terror, murder, bloodshed—but they produced Michelangelo, Leonardo da Vinci, and the Renaissance.

In Switzerland, they had brotherly love, five hundred years of democracy and peace, and what did that produce? The cuckoo clock.

I learned, or Richard learned—we've forgotten who learned—that Graham Greene, who wrote the screenplay of *The Third Man*, only later published the preliminary treatment as a novella, and the cuckoo-clock speech does not appear either in the novella or in the original screenplay. Greene did not write it. Orson Welles thought it up and said it.

After the Swiss Army piece appeared in *The New Yorker*, I expected a swarm of letters containing nits that only a Swiss could pick. Those *New Yorker* issues (October 31 and November 7, 1983) were read in Switzerland more widely than I ever would have guessed. Some months later, the book that reprinted them sold well there, too, actually reaching very high on the national list, the fact notwithstanding that the book was in English. Yet as a result of Richard's fact-checking no word has ever come to me from Switzerland (or, for that matter, from anywhere else) of an error in the English version. The French version was done by two translators for a publisher in Paris. A hundred and forty errors were found in it by the adjutant François Rumpf, who fixed them himself for a second printing.

Richard Sacks moved on from *The New Yorker* to *Reader's Digest* and has retired from the *Digest* to the lone preoccupations of a novelist. I told him recently how impressed I continue to be that in more than a third of a century no Swiss has sent a corrective letter about that story.

This fact did not check out with Richard. "Oh, but there was one letter," he said. "Something about a German word, but the reader was wrong."

•

In a 1993 essay on Sylvia Plath and Ted Hughes and the three decades of biographies that had described them, Janet Malcolm mentioned a plaque on the house in London where Plath was living with her two children when she died. The galley proof said:

> Olwyn and I finally reached the house on Fitzroy Road where Plath killed herself. I recognized it immediately— it is an obligatory photographic subject of the Plath biographies, and its oval blue ceramic plaque reading "William Butler Yeats, 1865–1939, Irish poet and dramatist, lived here" is a compulsively mentioned (and yet oddly irrelevant) detail.

"Irrelevant" is not a word that travels far in the checking department. The checker called *The New Yorker*'s London office, a species of exaggeration where three and sometimes four people worked on an upper floor in an old building in Hay Hill, Mayfair. One was a young English cyclist named Matt Seaton, whose title was London Bureau Manager. Now a columnist for *The Guardian*, Seaton vividly remembers the call about the plaque: "The checker was very specific in requesting that I actually go see it to ascertain that it was indeed blue and ceramic (as opposed to, say, black enamel tin). . . . I found the errand slightly absurd/amusing, because if you live in London you know there are plaques like this all over, and they're all basically the same." Seaton, nevertheless, descended the stairs, got on his bicycle, and went via Portland Place to the outer circle road around Regent's Park and then up Primrose Hill to 23 Fitzroy to check the Yeats plaque.

In the nineteen-eighties, Michelle Preston checked a piece on the iconography of New York City street signs. She went out and looked at the signs and "just about all of them were wrong."

The signs weren't wrong; the writer was; and the piece was O.K. because the facts could be professionally corrected. Less easily realigned was a checking proof in which the writer bushwhacked uphill through wild terrain to a certain summit in the Appalachians. The checker went to the mountain and found that she could drive to the top. If a writer writes that Santa Claus went down a chimney wearing a green suit, the color will be challenged, and the checker will try to learn Santa's waist measurement and the chimney's interior dimensions. Not only is fiction checked but also cartoon captions and the drawings themselves. When two cars passing an American gas station were each driving on the left side of the road, a checker noticed. The image had been flipped in reproduction.

Humor is checked in all forms, sometimes causing fact-checkers to be cast as obtuse. Joshua Hersh was not fond of this hair shirt. "We understand humor; we are real people," he asserts. "But we have to ask: 'Do you mean this humorously? Is that a joke or a mistake?'"

It could be both. In a piece called "Farewell to the Nineteenth Century"—which described the Kennebec River now, then, and earlier—I mentioned that the schooner Hesperus was built in Hallowell, Maine, downstream of Augusta. I said that the Hesperus had been "wrecked multiguously by Henry Wadsworth Longfellow." The fact-checker looked into it. Then—in a tone that was a wee bit stern and adversarial, not to mention critical—she said to me: "Longfellow did not wreck the Hesperus!"

I was surprised to be told by Richard Sacks that The New Yorker once checked people's claims and anecdotes and so forth only with the source, and not—or not as a rule, anyway—with third parties. If someone said he was Jerome Kern's cousin, he was Jerome Kern's cousin, tick, tick, tick. The fact-checkers certainly triangulate now. If three sources tell the same story, there is a reasonable probability that under enough additional inquiry it may be thought correct. Today's fact-checkers always start with the Internet, they tell me, and then ramify through the New York Public Library and beyond— a pilgrimage from the errant to the trustworthy. In the nineteen-sixties, acting within some legislated legalese known as "the mining exception," Kennecott Copper planned an open pit in the Glacier Peak Wilderness of the North Cascades. The Sierra Club said the mine would be visible from the moon. With the additional counsel of planetary scientists, the checking department decided that it would not be.

When the novelist Susan Diamond was a fact-checker at *The New Yorker*, she called a number in San Francisco one day, and said, "Is this the city water department?"

Voice on phone: "No. This is Acme Air Conditioning."

Susan: [*pause*] "Well, perhaps you can help me."

Overhearing bits of conversation was not a feat. The departmental space at 25 West Forty-third Street, where *The New Yorker* spent the fifty-six years ending in 1991, was basically one room in which seven desks were tightly packed among piled books and tumbling paper. Easily traversable in five steps, it closely resembled the communications center in George Washington's headquarters at Valley Forge, where twenty officers in a twelve-by-twelve-foot room sat all day long writing letters. Sara remembers a German fact-checker named Helga, who was "spiffy-looking, with long hair." When Kennedy Fraser wrote a piece on a furniture store, calling its furniture "ersatz," Helga called the store. "Tell me," she said. "Do you have any ersatz furniture?" Dusty Mortimer-Maddox, a great checker who held the job for almost as many years as Martin Baron, at one point had a fur-covered telephone. In the room on Forty-third Street, a cruciform emblem said "God Bless Our Home." After Jewish checkers objected, the cross was put on the department's reference Bible. When the magazine crossed the street, in 1991, the cross crossed with it. When the magazine moved to Times Square, in 1999, the cross went to the Crossroads of the World. Twice as many checkers now work in three times as much space as the department had at 25 West Forty-third Street. Martin Baron has been through every scene described. He is a fact-checker so learned in the procedures of scholarship that an editor once said to me, "Always remember this about Martin: he is never wrong." This was not a character judgment. It was just a checkable fact. Martin was checking a story by Ken Auletta on the day that Auletta married the literary agent Amanda "Binky" Urban. Shortly before the ceremony, Martin was in Ken and Binky's apartment, with galley proofs, checking facts with the groom. And more facts. The bride was on the roof, sunbathing. When she came down, she said, "Martin, I love you, but you have to go now because we have to get married."

Robert Bingham, gone since 1982, was an author's editor of the highest rank and the executive editor of the magazine. With Sara Lippincott, he devised a checker test. Sara described it, in part, when she spoke to the aspiring journalists: "What we want are people who . . . already know that there are nine men in a batting order, what a Republican is, and that the Earth is the third planet from the sun. That being got past, it helps if you speak French, German, Spanish, Italian, and Russian, read classical Greek, have low blood pressure, love your fellow man, and don't have to leave town on weekends." The checker test was a great deal more challenging than the examples Sara gives. It was the sort of thing Republican presidents routinely flunk. Who is the Sultan of Oman? Who is the Emir of Qatar? Who is the King of Bhutan? Who is the Secretary of Health and Human Services? What is acetylsalicylic acid? Last night, where was the Dow? (That last one was Bingham's way of assessing poets.) Over time, as new candidates came along, the test was updated and modified. When Michelle Preston came along, in the nineteen-eighties, she achieved the checker test's highest all-time score. Like her husband, Richard Preston, she is now a *New Yorker* contributor.

•

In the comfortable knowledge that the fact-checking department is going to follow up behind me, I like to guess at certain names and numbers early on, while I change and re-change and listen to sentences, preferring to hear some ballpark figure or approximate date than the dissonant clink of journalistic terms: WHAT CITY, $000,000, name TK, number TK, Koming. These are forms of promissory note and a checker is expected to pay it. Koming means what koming sounds like and is sort of kute; TK means "to come." At least for me, they don't serve the sound of a drafted sentence as well as flat-out substitutes, pro-tem inventions. In a freight train a mile and a half long, there is a vital tube of air that runs the full length and controls the brakes. In "Coal Train" (2005), I felt a need for analogy and guessed at one:

> The releasing of the air brakes began at the two ends, and moved toward the middle. The train's very long integral air tube was like the air sac of an American eel.

Before long the checking department was up to its chin in ichthyologists, and I was informed by Josh Hersh that the air sac of an American eel is proportionally a good deal shorter than the air sac in most ordinary fish.
"Who says so?"
"Willy Bemis."
"Oh."

Willy Bemis is to the anatomy of fishes what Eldridge Moores is to tectonics. Willy was the central figure in a book of mine that had been published three years before, parts of which appeared in *The New Yorker.* He had since left the University of Massachusetts to become the director of Shoals Marine Laboratory, the offshore classrooms of Cornell University and the University of New Hampshire. I called him in Ithaca to ask what could be done. Ever accommodating, Willy at first tried to rationalize the eel. Maybe its air sac was up to the job after all. Maybe the analogy would work. I said the eel would never make it through the checking department, or, for that matter, past me. We were close to closing, and right offhand Willy was unable to think of a species with a long enough sac. What to do? What else? He called Harvard. The train's very long integral air tube was like the air sac of a rope fish.

•

On the Merrimack River in Merrimack, New Hampshire, is a Budweiser brewery that brewed its first Bud in 1970. In 1839, John and Henry Thoreau passed the site in their homemade skiff on the journey that resulted in Henry's first book. A run of white water there had been known as Cromwell's Falls since the seventeenth century, but, Thoreau wrote, "these falls are the Nesenkeag of the Indians," and he went on to say, "Great Nesenkeag Stream comes in on the right just above." New Hampshire has a number of place names that end in the letters "k e a g." The "keag" is pronounced as if the "a" were missing; i.e., "keg." In 2003, my son-in-law Mark Svenvold and I went through Nesenkeag Falls and Namaskeag Falls and Amoskeag Falls, in an Old Town canoe, tracing the Thoreaus' upstream journey, and while dragging the canoe up the rapids I found myself wondering how many kegs that Budweiser plant could produce in a day. Back home and writing, I made up a number out of thin air, and it is what Anne Stringfield, checking the facts, saw on her proof:

> Just above Cromwell's Falls on Route 3, very close to but not visible from the river, is a Budweiser brewery that has a production average of thirteen thousand kegs a day.

> Never underestimate Anheuser-Busch. The average production turned out to be eighteen thousand kegs a day.

•

Another fluvial piece—"Tight-Assed River"—was checked by Josh Hersh in 2004. He found this on his proof:

> People say, "The Illinois River? What's that? Never heard of it. Where does it go?" Actually, there are two Illinois Rivers in America, each, evidently, as well known as the other.

> One is in Illinois, another is in Arkansas and Oklahoma; and those two are all you will find in Merriam-Webster's Geographical Dictionary, which is among the checking department's more revered references. Josh dove into the Web, and came up with a third—an Illinois River in Oregon, which is not well known even in Oregon.

> Actually, there are three Illinois Rivers in America, each, evidently, as well known as the others.

> (More recently, before this chapter appeared in *The New Yorker*, the fact-checking department found yet another Illinois River—in Colorado. If I were to republish this bit of fluvial information forty-six more times, evidently we would find an Illinois River in every state in the Union.)

That feat, on Josh's part, was just a stretching exercise before he took on, among other things, a cabin boat that was drifting idly on the eponymous Illinois while a vessel longer than an aircraft carrier bore down upon it sounding five short blasts, the universal statement of immediate danger. The vessel, more than eleven hundred feet long and wired rigid, was made up of fifteen barges pushed by a "towboat." I was in the pilothouse scribbling notes.

At just about the point where the cabin boat would go into our blind spot—the thousand feet of water that we in the pilothouse can't see—people appear on the cabin boat's deck, the boat starts up, and in a manner that seems both haughty and defiant moves slowly and slightly aside. We grind on downriver as the boat moves up to pass us port to port, making its way up the thousand feet of barges to draw even with the pilothouse. Two men and two women are in the cabin boat. The nearest woman—seated left rear in the open part of the cockpit— is wearing a black-and-gold two-piece bathing suit. She has the sort of body you go to see in marble. She has golden hair. Quickly, deftly, she reaches with both hands behind her back and unclasps her top. Setting it on her lap, she swivels ninety degrees to face the tow-boat square. Shoulders back, cheeks high, she holds her pose without retreat. In her ample presentation there is defiance of gravity. There is no angle of repose. She is a siren and these are her songs.

So far so checkable. Something like that can be put—in newyorkerspeak—"on author." It was my experience, my description, my construction, my erection. No one seemed worried about the color of the bathing suit. I went on, though, to say something close to this:

She is Henry Moore's "Oval with Points." Moore said, "Rounded forms convey an idea of fruitfulness, maturity, probably because the earth, women's breasts, and most fruits are rounded, and these shapes are important because they have this background in our habits of perception. I think the humanist organic element will always be for me of fundamental importance in sculpture."

And now we were into deep checking. In 1975, I had telephoned Lynn Fraker, who was a docent for the art museum at Princeton, where Moore's "Oval with Points" is one of a couple of dozen very large and primarily abstract sculptures that stand outdoors around the campus. I wanted to use them as description exercises in my writing class, which I was about to teach for the first time. The Henry Moore, eleven feet tall, is shaped like a donut, and from each of its interior sides a conical and breastlike bulge extends toward another conical and breastlike bulge, their business ends nearly touching, as if they were on the ceiling of a chapel. It was my opinion that students should be able to do a better description than that. "Donut," for example, was not a word that should be allowed to rise into the company of Henry Moore; and in every class I have taught since then I have used the notes from that talk with Lynn Fraker. They include the words of Henry Moore, which she recited from memory. And now in 2004 I had no idea where she read them. She had left Princeton decades before, had remarried, and was at that time unreachable.

The Internet was no help, but Josh, searching through the catalogues of the New York Public Library, learned that collections of Moore's commentaries on sculptural art were in a midtown branch, across Fifth Avenue from the library's main building. After an hour or two there, he found an essay by Moore from a 1937 issue of the BBC's *The Listener*. In the next-to-last paragraph were the words that Lynn Fraker had rattled off to me. They needed very little adjustment to be rendered verbatim, as they are above. After which, we were back to "on author":

> She has not moved—this half-naked Maja outnakeding the whole one. Her nipples are a pair of eyes staring the towboat down. For my part, I want to leap off the tow, swim to her, and ask if there is anything I can do to help.

•

Perhaps I am giving the fact-checkers too much credit. After all, I do what they do before they do. I don't leave a mountain of work to them, and this is especially true if *The New Yorker* has rejected the piece and I am forging ahead to include it in a book, as happened in 2002, when the magazine turned a cold eye—for some inexplicable reason—on twelve thousand words about the American history of a fish. So I checked the virginal parts of the book myself, risking analogy with the lawyer who defends himself and has a fool for a client. The task took me three months—trying to retrace the facts in the manuscript by as many alternate routes as I could think of, as fact-checkers routinely do. There were a couple of passages that slowed things down almost to a halt, when, for one reason or another, it took eons on the Internet and more time in libraries to determine what to do or not to do.

> Penn's daughter Margaret fished in the Delaware, and wrote home to a brother asking him to "buy for me a four joynted strong fishing Rod and Real with strong good Lines. . . ."

The problem was not with the rod or the real but with William Penn's offspring. Should there be commas around Margaret or no commas around Margaret? The presence or absence of commas would, in effect, say whether Penn had one daughter or more than one. The commas—there or missing there—were not just commas; they were facts, neither more nor less factual than the kegs of Bud or the color of Santa's suit. Margaret, one of Penn's several daughters, went into the book without commas. Moving on, I tried to check this one:

On Wednesday, August 15, 1716, near Cambridge, Massachusetts, Cotton Mather fell out of a canoe while fishing on Spy Pond. After emerging soaked, perplexed, fishless, he said, "My God, help me to understand the meaning of it!" Before long, he was chastising his fellow clerics for wasting God's time in recreational fishing. Not a lot of warmth there. Better to turn to the clergyman Fluviatulis Piscator, known to his family as Joseph Seccombe, who was twenty-one years old when Cotton Mather died. Beside the Merrimack River, in 1739, Piscator delivered a sermon that was later published as "A Discourse utter'd in Part at Ammauskeeg-Falls, in the Fishing Season." There are nine copies in existence. One was sold at auction in 1986 for fourteen thousand dollars. The one I saw was at the Library Company of Philadelphia. Inserted in it was a book dealer's description that said, "First American book on angling; first American publication on sports of field and stream. Seccombe's defense of fishing is remarkable for coming so early, in a time when fishing for fun needed defending."

There was, in all of that, one part of one sentence that proved, in 2002, exceptionally hard to check. It could easily have been rewritten in a different way, but I stubbornly wished to check it. To wit:

Joseph Seccombe, who was twenty-one years old when Cotton Mather died.

In order to tick those exact and unmodified words, you would need to know not only the year in which Mather died and the year in which Seccombe was born but also the month and day for each. When Mather died, on February 13, 1728, Seccombe was either twenty-one or twenty-two. Which? The Internet failed me. Libraries failed me. The complete works of Joseph Seccombe and Fluviatulis Piscator failed me. I called Kingston, New Hampshire, where he had served as minister for more than twenty years. The person I reached there generously said she would look through town and church records and call me back, which she did, two or three days later. She was sorry. She had looked long and hard, but in Kingston evidently the exact date of Seccombe's birth was nowhere to be found. I was about to give up and insert "in his early twenties" when a crimson lightbulb lit up in my head. If Joseph Seccombe was a minister in 1737 (the year he arrived in Kingston) he had been educated somewhere, and in those days in advanced education in the Province of Massachusetts Bay there was one game in town. I called Harvard.

By the main switchboard I was put through to someone who listened to my question and said right back, within a few seconds, "June 14, 1706."

Draft No. 4

Block. It puts some writers down for months. It puts some writers down for life. A not always brief or minor form of it mutes all writers from the outset of every day. "Dear Joel . . ." This is just a random sample from letters written to former students in response to their howling cries as they suffer the masochistic self-inflicted paralysis of a writer's normal routine. "Dear Joel . . ." This Joel will win huge awards and write countless books and a nationally syndicated column, but at the time of this letter he has just been finding out that to cross the electric fence from the actual world to the writing world requires at least as much invention as the writing itself. "Dear Joel: You are writing, say, about a grizzly bear. No words are forthcoming. For six, seven, ten hours no words have been forthcoming. You are blocked, frustrated, in despair. You are nowhere, and that's where you've been getting. What do you do? You write, 'Dear Mother.' And then you tell your mother about the block, the frustration, the ineptitude, the despair. You insist that you are not cut out to do this kind of work. You whine. You whimper. You outline your problem, and you mention that the bear has a fifty-five-inch waist and a neck more than thirty inches around but could run nose-to-nose with

Secretariat. You say the bear prefers to lie down and rest. The bear rests fourteen hours a day. And you go on like that as long as you can. And then you go back and delete the 'Dear Mother' and all the whimpering and whining, and just keep the bear."

You could be Joel, even if your name is Jenny. Or Julie, Jillian, Jim, Jane, Joe. You are working on a first draft and small wonder you're unhappy. If you lack confidence in setting one word after another and sense that you are stuck in a place from which you will never be set free, if you feel sure that you will never make it and were not cut out to do this, if your prose seems stillborn and you completely lack confidence, you must be a writer. If you say you see things differently and describe your efforts positively, if you tell people that you "just love to write," you may be delusional. How could anyone ever know that something is good before it exists? And unless you can identify what is not succeeding—unless you can see those dark clunky spots that are giving you such a low opinion of your prose as it develops—how are you going to be able to tone it up and make it work?

The idea of writing "Dear Mother" and later snipping off the salutation had popped into my head years ago while I was participating in a panel of writers at the Y in Princeton. Jenny was the only member of my family there. She was ten. The bear got a big laugh, but cheerlessly I also served up the masochism and the self-inflicted paralysis, causing Jenny to tell me afterward that I was not sketching a complete picture.

"You know it isn't all like that," she said. "You should tell about the good part."

She had a point. It isn't all like that—only the first draft. First drafts are slow and develop clumsily because every sentence affects not only those before it but also those that follow. The first draft of my book on California geology took two gloomy years; the second, third, and fourth drafts took about six months altogether. That four-to-one ratio in writing time—first draft versus the other drafts combined—has for me been consistent in projects of any length, even if the first draft takes only a few days or weeks. There are psychological differences from phase to phase, and the first is the phase of the pit and the pendulum. After that, it seems as if a different person is taking over. Dread largely disappears. Problems become less threatening, more interesting. Experience is more helpful, as if an amateur is being replaced by a professional. Days go by quickly and not a few could be called pleasant, I'll admit.

When Jenny was a senior at Princeton High School and much put out by the time it was taking her to start an assigned piece of writing, let alone complete it, she told me one day as I was driving her to school that she felt incompetent and was worried about the difficulty she was having getting things right the first time, worried by her need to revise. I went on to my office and wrote her a note. "Dear Jenny: The way to do a piece of writing is three or four times over, never once. For me, the hardest part comes first, getting something—anything—out in front of me. Sometimes in a nervous frenzy I just fling words as if I were flinging mud at a wall. Blurt out, heave out, babble out something—anything—as a first draft. With that, you have achieved a sort of nucleus. Then, as you work it over and alter it, you begin to shape sentences that score higher with the ear and eye. Edit it again—top to bottom. The chances are that about now you'll be seeing something that you are sort of eager for others to see. And all that takes time. What I have left out is the interstitial time. You finish that first awful blurt-ing, and then you put the thing aside. You get in your car and drive home. On the way, your mind is still knitting at the words. You think of a better way to say something, a good phrase to correct a certain problem. Without the drafted version—if it did not exist—you obviously would not be thinking of things that would improve it. In short, you may be actually writing only two or three hours a day, but your mind, in one way or another, is working on it twenty-four hours a day—yes, while you sleep—but only if some sort of draft or earlier version already exists. Until it exists, writing has not really begun."

The difference between a common writer and an improviser on a stage (or any performing artist) is that writing can be revised. Actually, the essence of the process is revision. The adulating portrait of the perfect writer who never blots a line comes Express Mail from fairyland.

Jenny grew up to write novels, and at this point has published three. She keeps everything close-hauled, says nothing and reveals nothing as she goes along. I once asked her if she had been thinking about starting another book, and she said, "I finished it last week." Her sister Martha, two years younger, has written four novels. Martha calls me up nine times a day to tell me that writing is impossible, that she's not cut out to do it, that she'll never finish what she is working on, et cetera, et cetera, and so forth and so on, and I, who am probably disintegrating a third of the way through an impossible first draft, am supposed to turn into the Rock of Gibraltar. The talking rock: "Just stay at it; perseverance will change things." "You're so unhappy you sound authentic to me." "You can't make a fix unless you know what is broken."

When Jenny was ten months out of college, she was beginning to develop some retrospective empathy for me on that day at the Y when she was ten. Now she was in Edinburgh, writing on a fellowship, and she told me in a letter of her continuing doubt and discouragement. Those were the days of paper airmail, and by paper airmail I replied.

With respect to her wish to become a writer, she said she was asking herself day after day, "Who am I kidding?"

I said, "I think I first started saying that to myself almost exactly forty years ago. Before that, when I was twelve, I had no such question. It just seemed dead easy—a rip, a scam—to tickle some machine and cause it to print money. I still ask myself, 'Who am I kidding?' Not long ago, that question seemed so pertinent to me that I would bury my head in my office pillow. I was undertaking to write about geology and the question was proper. Who was I to take on that subject? It was terrifying. One falls into such projects like slipping into caves, and then wonders how to get out. To feel such doubt is a part of the picture—important and inescapable. When I hear some young writer express that sort of doubt, it serves as a checkpoint; if they don't say something like it they are quite possibly, well, kidding themselves."

She said, "My style is always that of what I am reading at the time—or overwhelmingly self-conscious and strained."

I said, "How unfortunate that would be if you were fifty-four. At twenty-three, it is not only natural; it is important. The developing writer reacts to excellence as it is discovered—wherever and whenever—and of course does some imitating (unavoidably) in the process of drawing from the admired fabric things to make one's own. Rapidly, the components of imitation fade. What remains is a new element in your own voice, which is not in any way an imitation. Your manner as a writer takes form in this way, a fragment at a time. A style that lacks strain and self-consciousness is what you seem to aspire to, or you wouldn't be bringing the matter up. Therefore, your goal is in the right place. So practice taking shots at it. A relaxed, unselfconscious style is not something that one person is born with and another not. Writers do not spring full-blown from the ear of Zeus."

Jenny said, "I can't seem to finish anything."

I said, "Neither can I."

Then I went back to my own writing, my own inability to get going until five in the afternoon, my animal sense of being hunted, my resemblance to the sand of Gibraltar.

•

It is toward the end of the second draft, if I'm lucky, when the feeling comes over me that I have something I want to show to other people, something that seems to be working and is not going to go away. The feeling is more than welcome, but it is hardly euphoria. It's just a new lease on life, a sense that I'm going to survive until the middle of next month. After reading the second draft aloud, and going through the piece for the third time (removing the tin horns and radio static that I heard while reading), I enclose words and phrases in pencilled boxes for Draft No. 4. If I enjoy anything in this process it is Draft No. 4. I go searching for replacements for the words in the boxes. The final adjustments may be small-scale, but they are large to me, and I love addressing them. You could call this the copy-editing phase if real copy editors were not out there in the future prepared to examine the piece. The basic thing I do with college students is pretend that I'm their editor and their copy editor. In preparation for conferences with them, I draw boxes around words or phrases in the pieces they write. I suggest to them that they might do this for themselves.

You draw a box not only around any word that does not seem quite right but also around words that fulfill their assignment but seem to present an opportunity. While the word inside the box may be perfectly O.K., there is likely to be an even better word for this situation, a word right smack on the button, and why don't you try to find such a word? If none occurs, don't linger; keep reading and drawing boxes, and later revisit them one by one. If there's a box around "sensitive" because it seems pretentious in the context, try "susceptible." Why "susceptible"? Because you looked up "sensitive" in the dictionary and it said "highly susceptible." With dictionaries, I spend a great deal more time looking up words I know than words I have never heard of—at least ninety-nine to one. The dictionary definitions of words you are trying to replace are far more likely to help you out than a scattershot wad from a thesaurus. If you use the dictionary after the thesaurus, the thesaurus will not hurt you. So draw a box around "wad." Webster: "The cotton or silk obtained from the Syrian swallow-wort, formerly cultivated in Egypt and imported to Europe." Oh. But read on: "A little mass, tuft, or bundle . . . a small, compact heap." Stet that one. I call this "the search for the mot juste," because when I was in the eighth grade Miss Bartholomew told us that Gustave Flaubert walked around in his garden for days on end searching in his head for *le mot juste*. Who could forget that? Flaubert seemed heroic. Certain kids considered him weird.

This, for example, came up while I was writing about the Atchafalaya, the huge river swamp in southern Louisiana, and how it looked from a small plane in the air. Land is growing there as silt arrives from the north. Parts of the swamp are filling in. From the airplane, you could discern where these places were because, seen through the trees, there would be an interruption of the reflection of sunlight on water. What word or phrase was I going to use for that reflection? I looked up "sparkle" in my old Webster's Collegiate. It said: "See 'flash.'" I looked up "flash." The definitions were followed by a presentation of synonyms: "flash, gleam, glance, glint, sparkle, glitter, scintillate, coruscate, glimmer, shimmer mean to shoot forth light." I liked that last part, so I changed the manuscript to say, "The reflection of the sun races through the trees and shoots forth light from the water."

In the search for words, thesauruses are useful things, but they don't talk about the words they list. They are also dangerous. They can lead you to choose a polysyllabic and fuzzy word when a simple and clear one is better. The value of a thesaurus is not to make a writer seem to have a vast vocabulary of recondite words. The value of a thesaurus is in the assistance it can give you in finding the best possible word for the mission that the word is supposed to fulfill. Writing teachers and journalism courses have been known to compare them to crutches and to imply that no writer of any character or competence would use them. At best, thesauruses are mere rest stops in the search for the mot juste. Your destination is the dictionary. Suppose you sense an opportunity beyond the word "intention." You read the dictionary's thesaurian list of synonyms: "intention, intent, purpose, design, aim, end, object, objective, goal." But the dictionary doesn't let it go at that. It goes on to tell you the differences all the way down the line—how each listed word differs from all the others. Some dictionaries keep themselves trim by just listing synonyms and not going on to make distinctions. You want the first kind, in which you are not just getting a list of words; you are being told the differences in their hues, as if you were looking at the stripes in an awning, each of a subtly different green. Look up "vertical." It tells you— believe it or not—that "vertical," "perpendicular," and "plumb" differ each from the two others. Ditto "plastic, pliable, pliant, ductile, malleable, adaptable." Ditto "fidelity, allegiance, fealty, loyalty, devotion, piety."

I grew up in canoes on northern lakes and forest rivers. Thirty years later, I was trying to choose a word or words that would explain why anyone in a modern nation would choose to go a long distance by canoe. I was damned if I was going to call it a sport, but nothing else occurred. I looked up "sport." There were seventeen lines of definition: "1. That which diverts, and makes mirth; pastime; diversion. 2. A diversion of the field." I stopped there.

His professed criteria were to take it easy, see some wildlife, and travel light with his bark canoes—nothing more—and one could not help but lean his way. I had known of people who took collapsible cots, down pillows, chain saws, outboard motors, cases of beer, and battery-powered portable refrigerators on canoe trips—even into deep wilderness. You set your own standards. Travel by canoe is not a necessity, and will nevermore be the most efficient way to get from one region to another, or even from one lake to another—anywhere. A canoe trip has become simply a rite of oneness with certain terrain, a diversion of the field, an act performed not because it is necessary but because there is value in the act itself. . . .

If your journey is long enough in wild country, you change, albeit temporarily, while you are there. Writing about a river valley in Arctic Alaska, I was trying to describe that mental change, and I was searching for a word that would represent the idea, catalyze the theme. "Assimilate" came along pretty quickly. But "assimilate," in the context, was worse than "sport." So I looked up "assimilate": "1. To make similar or alike. 2. To liken; to compare. 3. "To . . . incorporate into the substance of the appropriating body."

We sat around the campfire for at least another hour. We talked of rain and kestrels, oil and antlers, the height and the headwaters of the river. Neither Hession nor Fedeler once mentioned the bear.

When I got into my sleeping bag, though, and closed my eyes, there he was, in color, on the side of the hill. The vision was indelible, but fear was not what put it there. More, it was a sense of sheer luck at having chosen in the first place to follow Fedeler and Hession up the river and into the hills—a memento not so much of one moment as of the entire circuit of the long afternoon. It was a vision of a whole land, with an animal in it. This was his country, clearly enough. To be there was to be incorporated, in however small a measure, into its substance—his country, and if you wanted to visit it you had better knock.

I was left, in time that followed, with one huge regret. In three years of Alaska travel, research, and writing, it never occurred to me to wonder why the Arctic was called Arctic. I never thought about it until a few years after the book was published. If only I had looked in the dictionary, I would have incorporated the word's origin into the substance of the writing. This is how "Arctic" is defined: "Pertaining to, or situated under, the northern constellation called the Bear."

•

It was William Shawn who first mentioned to me the "irregular restrictive 'which.'" Mr. Shawn explained that under certain unusual and special circumstances the word "which" could be employed at the head of a restrictive clause. Ordinarily, the conjunction "that" would introduce a restrictive clause. Nonrestrictive: This is a baseball, which is spherical and white. Restrictive: This is the baseball that Babe Ruth hit out of the park after pointing at the fence in Chicago. The first ball is unspecific, and the sentence requires a comma if the writer wishes to digress into its shape and color. The second ball is very specific, and the sentence repels commas. There can be situations, though, wherein words or phrases lie between the specific object and the clause that proves its specificity, and would call for the irregular restrictive "which."

Confronting this memory, I cannot say that it kicks old Buddha's gong. Yet it has sent me through the entirety of two of my books on a computer search for the irregular restrictive "which." In well over a hundred thousand words, I found three:

In 1822, the Belgian stratigrapher J. J. d'Omalius d'Halloy, working for the French government, put a name on the chalk of Europe which would come to represent an ungainly share of geologic time.

Oakmont uses a *Poa annua* of its own creation which bears few seeds and therefore results in what golfers describe as a "less pebbly" surface.

Dominy had risen to become U.S. Commissioner of Reclamation, the agency in the Department of the Interior which impounds water for as much as two hundred miles behind such constructions as Glen Canyon Dam, Grand Coulee Dam, Flaming Gorge Dam, Hoover Dam.

As it happens, those excerpts are not from the Shawn era but are all from pieces published in the twenty-first century. *The New Yorker*, in other words, has by no means forgotten the irregular restrictive "which," or the regular earth from which it springs.

In the same books, incidentally, I also quoted Thoreau and Leviticus, and may have winced in Shawn's honor.

Four hundred yards above the interstate bridge, we came to Carthagina Island, standing in a flat-water pool. Thoreau doesn't call it by name, but he describes it as "a large and densely wooded island . . . the fairest which we had met with, with a handsome grove of elms at its head."

Nothing irregular there, H.D.T. It was the fairest island that you met with.

Leviticus: "And the Lord spake unto Moses and to Aaron, saying unto them, Speak unto the children of Israel, saying, These are the beasts which ye shall eat among all the beasts that are on the earth."

Actually, Mr. Shawn was just another spear-carrier in the hall of usage and grammar. The dais was occupied for more than half a century by Eleanor Gould, "Miss Gould," who was Mrs. Packard, and whose wide reputation seeped down even into the awareness of apprentice writers everywhere. I was scarcely eighteen, and already collecting rejection slips, when I heard or read about a twenty-two-year-old Vassar graduate named Eleanor Gould, who, in 1925, bought a copy of the brand-new *New Yorker*, read it, and then reread it with a blue pencil in her hand. When she finished, the magazine was a mottled blue on every page—a circled embarrassment of dangling modifiers, conflicting pronouns, absent commas, and over-all grammatical hash. She mailed the marked-up copy to Harold Ross, the founding editor, and Ross was said to have bellowed. What he bellowed was "Find this bitch and hire her!"

In reality, Eleanor Gould was nine years old when Ross invented *The New Yorker*. She grew up in Ohio, went to Oberlin College, and graduated in 1938. Seven years later, she sought a job at *The New Yorker*, and in her application she mentioned one or two examples of the sort of help she felt she could provide. For example, something is not different *than* something else; it is different *from* something else. It was Shawn who hired her. He was the managing editor. There is no compact or simple title for what she did across the following fifty-four years. She was not an editor—not, at any rate, on the higher levels of holding writers' hands. She was not a fact-checker, although she would surely mention any fact that struck her as suspect. What she did was read the magazine in galley proofs and mark up the proofs. Each galley had a *New Yorker* column running down the middle and enough margin on either side to park a car. She filled the margins with remarks about usage, diction, indirection, word choice, punctuation, ambiguities, and so forth. Her completed product was sent on to the writer's editor, who read the marginalia and later brought up selected items with the writer, or just handed the writer the Gould proof, as it was known, and let the writer soak it up. Robert Bingham always passed the Gould proof along to me, almost always saying, "When she says 'Grammar,' sit up!"

On a highly competitive list, her foremost peeve in factual writing was indirection—sliding facts in sideways, expecting a reader to gather rather than receive information. You don't start off like an atmospheric fictionist: "The house on Lovers' Lane was where the lovers loved loving." A Gould proof would have asked, "What house?" "What lovers?" "Where is Lovers' Lane?" In short, if you are introducing something, introduce it. Don't get artistic with the definite article. If you say "a house," you are introducing it. If you say "the house," the reader knows about it because you mentioned it earlier. Mr. Shawn was influenced by Miss Gould far more than vice versa. He was a bear on indirection.

Her suggested fixes did not always rise into comparison with invisible mending. Some writers developed reactions in the tantrum range. Nothing, though, was being forced upon the prose. If the writer wished to ignore a salient comment from Miss Gould instead of slapping the forehead and feeling grateful, that was up to the writer. It was the writer's signed piece. If the writer preferred warts, warts prevailed. A Gould proof rarely endeavored to influence in any manner the structure or thesis of a piece, and was not meant to. Its purpose, according to Miss Gould, was to help a writer achieve an intent in the clearest possible way. She sat you up, let me tell you. And not only did you not have to accept her suggested fixes but also— of course—you were free to fix the fixes according to the sound of things in your own head.

The general term for all this—from "house style" to a Gould-like proof—is "copy editing." Miss Gould accepted the title "grammarian" for several decades, but grammar was only the base of things she reacted to as she monitored the magazine. House style was actually dealt with by others before she saw anything. House style is not a reference to the canard that an entire magazine can be made to sound as if it were written by one writer. House style is a mechanical application of things like spelling and italics. In *The New Yorker*, "travelling" is spelled with two "l"s. Book titles are framed in quotation marks. The names of magazines are italicized, and if the names are in the possessive—*TV Guide's*, *National Geographic's*—the "s" is italicized, too. The names of ships are not italicized. It is house style to put the two dots over a second consecutive identical vowel because the house does not coöperate in deëmphasizing diaereses. In articles in *The New York Times* the name of everybody mentioned is preceded by Mr., Ms., or Mrs. (if not by a lofty title like President, Senator, General, or Cardinal), and, traditionally, if a *Times* reporter got into a skin boat with an Eskimo in the Chukchi Sea no personal pronoun was ever going to get into that boat. "A visitor" got into that boat. *The Chicago Manual of Style* is a quixotic attempt at one-style-fits-all for every house in America—newspapers, magazines, book publishers, blogishers.

Copy editors attend the flow of the prose and watch for leaks. Whatever else she was called, Eleanor Gould was a copy editor. She was one of several in a developing tradition that became a legacy. For a single closing issue, today's copy editors read *New Yorker* proofs so many times and in so many ways that they variously subtitle their own efforts. The five incumbents call themselves copy editors, page O.K.'ers, query proofreaders, and second readers. They all do all of it, and that's four job descriptions each for five people—twenty functionaries at five desks. They also do what Eleanor Gould did, and to this day when they finish working on a galley proof they say that it has been "Goulded." If they live in her shadow, they lengthen it.

They can be rarefied. Reading a sentence like "She didn't know what happened to the other five people travelling with her," they will see that what the writer could mean is that the traveller was one of eleven people on the trip. This is high-alloy nitpicking, but why not? There is elegance in the less ambiguous way. She didn't know what happened to the five other people who were travelling with her.

To linger in the same thin air, what is the difference between "further" and "farther"? In the dictionary, look up "further." It says "farther." Look up "farther." It says "further." So you're safe and can roll over and sleep. But the distinction has a difference and O.K.'ers know what's O.K. "Farther" refers to measurable distance. "Further" is a matter of degree. Will you stop pelting me with derision? That's enough out of you. You'll go no further.

Getting into an authentic standoff with this multitalented, multifaceted, proofreading, query-proofing, copy-editing, grammar-wielding corps is difficult to do, and in fifty years I have done so twice. One standoff, which shall not be elaborated here, had to do with my flippant use of scholarly parenthetical in-text citations (Mourt, 1622) in a piece in which the works cited did not appear on what scholars call the works-cited list. There was no works-cited list. The other standoff—related to the issue of February 23, 1987—had to do with the possessive of the word Corps. It was the piece about southern Louisiana, the Atchafalaya River, the vast swamp, and the levees, spillways, and navigation locks of the U.S. Army Corps of Engineers. It approached twenty thousand words in length and, as you can imagine, the word Corps was all over the text like an eruption of measles. Often, the word occurred in the possessive. When I was in the eighth grade, Miss Bartholomew told us that a noun ending in "s" could be rendered possessive by an apostrophe alone or by an apostrophe followed by an additional "s," tie goes to the writer. Now, in the Louisiana piece, I had written Corps' for each and every possessive Corps, and the copy editors said that the possessive of Corps should be printed as Corps's. I thought I was in a morgue. I said so. The copy editors phalanxed—me versus the whole department. They said that *The New Yorker* did not use the naked "s" apostrophe except with classical names like Jesus, Aeschylus, and Socrates; and even French names ending in a silent "s" were given the apostrophe "s," as in "François's," "*les jeunesses's*," "Epesses's"—also as in "Amiens's hidden cache" and "*le français's* frank mustache." With regard to Corps's, the copy editors were uncharacteristically unbending. I said that if Corps's had to be the form printed, I would have to stop all forward motion and rewrite every sentence in which that possessive occurred—in ways that would avoid using it, in ways that would get rid of "all those corpses." I'm sure I spluttered about "slabsful of recumbents" and said it would be "as if every one of those Corps's was wired to a cold toe." This threat was not considered persuasive, but eventually it led to someone's remarkable suggestion. Why not call the U.S. Army Corps of Engineers and ask what they do when they need to express themselves in the possessive? I hadn't known that the Army Corps of Engineers was steeped in *Fowler's Modern English Usage* or Merriam-Webster's unparalleled *English Usage* or the flexibilities of grammar. How would the Corps write it? Corps', said the Corps. Never Corps's. Never the geminal "s"s.

Copy editors seldom stray into the realms of others, but when they do, their suggestions and comments are not unwelcome. Mary Norris, who joined *The New Yorker* in 1978 and has worked on untold numbers of my pieces, is a verbal diagnostician I would turn to for a first, second, or third opinion on just about anything. She doesn't mind when friends call her the Pencil Lady. A blog she began on *The New Yorker's* Web site, mostly about copy-editing, evolved into the best-selling book *Between You & Me: Confessions of a Comma Queen*

(Norton, 2015). In 2003, we were closing the piece that retraced the journey made in 1839 by Henry David Thoreau and his brother, John, down the Concord River to the Merrimack and up the Merrimack through and beyond Manchester, New Hampshire. In manuscript and in the initial galley proofs, there was a sentence (odd out of context) that said:

> In bed at night for three or four months I'd been listening to Manchester laughing—a chorus of Manchesterians sitting on those steps convulsed by us on the way uphill with our canoe.

Mary Norris wrote on the proof, "Would you like 'Mancunians'?"

It was as if she had handed me a rare gold coin. Five years later, when I happened to be writing about lacrosse in Manchester, England, I worked in the word "Mancunian" three times in one short paragraph. It was the second-best demonym I'd ever heard, almost matching Vallisoletano (a citizen of Valladolid). The planet, of course, is covered with demonyms, and after scouring the world in conversations on this topic with Mary Norris I began a severely selective, highly subjective A-list, extending Mancunian and Vallisoletano through thirty-five others at this writing, including Wulfrunian (Wolverhampton), Novocastrian (Newcastle), Trifluvian (Trois-Rivières), Leodensian (Leeds), Minneapolitan (Minneapolis), Hartlepudlian (Hartlepool), Liverpudlian (you knew it), Haligonian (Halifax), Varsovian (Warsaw), Providentian (Providence), and Tridentine (Trent).

•

One can do worse than pretend to be a copy editor. In my role as my students' editor, I go through their papers with them privately a comma at a time. Much of what I tell them I have learned by osmosis from those O.K. O.K.'ers at *The New Yorker*, not to mention a range of others, from Miss Bartholomew, of Princeton Junior High School, to Carmen Gomezplata, of Farrar, Straus and Giroux. The students, picking up the parlance, sometimes go off and copy-edit their roommates. This has led to disputes, and I have been asked to settle the disputes. My name isn't Strunk. I'm just another editee. But I do what I can, as, for example, after two such people recently got into a squabble over—imagine this—the possessive plural of "attorney general." The question came to me in an e-mail: "If more than one attorney general possess a number of cars, how would you fill in the blanks (if at all) in the following sentence: 'the attorney[] general[] car[] were all parked next to one another'?"

Both Web II and Random House say flatly that the plural of "attorney general" is both "attorneys general" and "attorney generals." That being so, I put on my robe, rapped the gavel, and said from the bench, "If you accept that the two forms are equal, I think you would write attorney generals' cars and not attorneys general's cars—for obvious reasons (a sense of the sight and sound of words has to kick in somewhere or the writer is missing one or two marbles)." What would I personally do? None of the above. I would refer to "the cars of the attorneys general." But that's just a matter of choice.

I work in a fake medieval turret on the roof of a campus building. When I come out and walk around, bumping into friends, they tend to ask me, "What are you working on?" Which is one reason I don't often come out and walk around. I always feel like a parrot answering that question, and a nervous ill-humored parrot if I am writing a first draft. A few years ago, I had the luxury of a one-word reply.

"What are you working on?"

"Chalk."

"Chalk?"

"Chalk."

That did it. That seemed to be one more syllable than any-one wished to pursue.

But when the question comes in a note from one of your own daughters it is wise not to wax monosyllabic. Jenny, for example, was an assistant editor at Alfred A. Knopf when she innocently asked what I was working on, and got this reply:

"Dear Jenny: What am I working on? How is it going? Since you asked, at this point I have no confidence in this piece of writing. It tries a number of things I probably shouldn't be trying. It tries to use the present tense for the immediacy that the present tense develops, but without allowing any verb tense to become befouled in a double orientation of time. It tells its story inside out. Like the ship I'm writing about, it may have a crack in its hull. And I've barely started. After four months and nine days of staring into this monitor for what has probably amounted in aggregate to something closely approach-ing a thousand hours, that's enough. I'm going fishing."

Omission

At *Time* magazine in the nineteen-fifties, the entry-level job for writers was a column called Miscellany. Filled with one-sentence oddities culled from newspapers and the wire services, Miscellany ran down its third of a page like a ladder, each wee story with its own title—traditionally, and almost invariably, a pun. Writers did not long endure there, and were not meant to, but just after I showed up a hiring freeze shut the door behind me and I wrote Miscellany for a year and a half. That came to roughly a thousand one-sentence stories, a thousand puns.

I am going to illustrate this with one, and only one, example. A person riding a bicycle on a street in Detroit fell asleep at the handlebars. My title was "Two Tired."

If a writer were ever to look back on many decades of pun-free prose, Miscellany was a good place to be when you were young. Words are too easy to play on. When I joined *The New Yorker*, in 1965, I left puns behind. Not that I have never suffered a relapse. In the nineteen-seventies, I turned in a manuscript containing a pun so fetid I can't remember it. My editor then was Robert Bingham, who said, "We should take that out."

The dialogue that followed became part of a remembrance of him:

I said, "A person has a right to make a pun once in a while, and even to be a little coarse." He said, "The line is not on the level of the rest of the piece and therefore seems out of place." I said, "That may be, but I want it in there." He said, "Very well. It's your piece." Next day, he said, "I think I ought to tell you I haven't changed my mind about that. It's an unfortunate line." I said, "Listen, Bobby. We discussed that. It's funny. I want to use it. If I'm embarrassing anybody, I'm embarrassing myself." He said, "O.K. I just work here." The day after that, I came in and said to him, "That joke. Let's take that out. I think that ought to come out." "Very well," he said, with no hint of triumph in his eye.

William Shawn, after editing my first two pieces himself, turned me over to Bingham very soon after Bingham came to *The New Yorker* from *The Reporter*, where he had been the managing editor. I was a commuter and worked more at home than at the magazine. I had not met, seen, or even heard of Bingham when Shawn gave him the manuscript of my forty-thousand-word piece called "Oranges."

A year earlier, I had asked Mr. Shawn if he thought oranges would be a good subject for a piece of nonfiction writing. In his soft, ferric voice, he said, "Oh." After a pause, he said, "Oh, yes." And that was all he said. But it was enough. As a "staff writer," I was basically an unsalaried freelance, and I left soon for Florida on his nickel. Why oranges? There was a machine in Pennsylvania Station that cut and squeezed them. I stopped there as routinely as an animal at a salt lick. Across the winter months, I thought I noticed a change in the color of the juice, light to deep, and I had also seen an ad somewhere that showed what appeared to be four identical oranges, although each had a different name. My intention in Florida was to find out why, and write a piece that would probably be short for *New Yorker* nonfiction of that day—something under ten thousand words. In Polk County, at Lake Alfred, though, I happened into the University of Florida's Citrus Experiment Station, five buildings isolated within vast surrounding groves. Several dozen people in those buildings had Ph.D.s in oranges, and there was a citrus library of a hundred thousand titles—scientific papers mainly, and doctoral dissertations, and six thousand books. Then and there, my project magnified. Back home, and many months later, I sent in the manuscript. Mr. Shawn accepted it, indicating gently that it might need a little squeezing itself before publication.

Mr. Shawn seems to have instructed Mr. Bingham to hunt for a few galleys' worth of information and throw the rest away. At any rate, what reached me in New Jersey was more than shocking. The envelope was large but thinner than a postcard. After glancing through Bingham's condensation, I called the office, asked if I could see Mr. Shawn, got on a train, and went to the city. Shawn was even smaller than I am, which is getting down there, but after going past his moats and entering his presence you were looking across a desk at an intimidating sovereign. Pathetically, I blurted out, "Mr. Bingham has removed eighty-five per cent of what I wrote?"

Shawn (incredulous, innocent, saucer-eyed): "He has?"

I responded affirmatively.

He said perhaps I should have a conversation with Mr. Bingham. He would arrange it. Mary Painter, his quiet Cerberus, would be in touch with me.

Five days later, I returned to the city to meet Mr. Bingham. I remember hating him as I drank my juice in Penn Station. In Florida in orange-juice-concentrate plants, there was a machine made by the Food Machinery Corporation called the short-form extractor. I thought of Bingham as the short-form extractor and would call him that from time to time for years. He came down the hall to an office I had at the magazine, in a row of writers' tiny spaces that one writer called Sleepy Hollow. This man who came through my doorway was agreeable-looking, actually handsome, with a bright-blue gaze, an oscillating bow tie, curly light-brown hair, and a sincere mustache—an instantly likable guy if the instant had not been this one. He said he was not sure how to begin our conversation, but he wondered if I would prefer to add things back to the proof that was sent to me or start with the original manuscript and talk about what might be left out.

He talked with me for five days. Enough of the manuscript was restored to make a serial publication that ran in two issues, but by no means all of it was restored. Citrus is citrus first and Sweet Orange of Valencia or Washington Navel second. The sex life of citrus is spectacular. Plant a lime seed and up comes a kumquat, or, with equal odds, a Seville orange, not to mention a rough lemon or a tangerine. "Character Differences Among Seedlings of the Persian Lime" was the title of the scientific paper that described all that—a perfect title for anybody's seven-hundred-page family history, and one item among many that expanded my manuscript to the size it reached as themes spread into related themes.

Writing is selection. Just to start a piece of writing you have to choose one word and only one from more than a million in the language. Now keep going. What is your next word? Your next sentence, paragraph, section, chapter? Your next ball of fact. You select what goes in and you decide what stays out. At base you have only one criterion: If something interests you, it goes in—if not, it stays out. That's a crude way to assess things, but it's all you've got. Forget market research. Never market-research your writing. Write on subjects in which you have enough interest on your own to see you through all the stops, starts, hesitations, and other impediments along the way.

Ideally, a piece of writing should grow to whatever length is sustained by its selected material—that much and no more.

Many, if not most, of my projects have begun as ideas for *The New Yorker's* section called The Talk of the Town, and many of them have grown to greater length. In the nineteen-seventies, observing the trials of an experimental aircraft, I intended at first to tell the story in a thousand words, but the tests and trials increased in number, changed, went on for years; a rich stream of characters happened through the scene; and the unfolding story had a natural structure analogous to a dramatic plot. The ultimate piece ran at fifty-five thousand words in three consecutive issues of the magazine. "Oranges," seven years earlier, had grown in the same way, but my aptitude for selection needed growing, too. Bingham, after restoring much of what he had cut (and suggesting to Shawn that what we were doing made sense), insisted that substantial amounts of text remain down and out. Even I could see that for magazine purposes he was right. Four or five months later, as the piece was being prepared for publication as a book, I asked my close friend Mr. Bingham to help me choose from the original manuscript what else to restore, and what not to restore, to the text. In other words, the library at the Citrus Experiment Station had beguiled me so much—not to mention the citrus scientists, the growers, the rich kings of juice concentration—that I lost the advantage of what is left out.

•

Anne Fadiman, whose 1997 book, *The Spirit Catches You and You Fall Down: A Hmong Child, Her American Doctors, and the Collision of Two Cultures,* won the National Book Critics Circle Award and is a demonstration of the potentialities of nonfiction writing, teaches her craft at Yale. Some years ago, she e-mailed various writers she knew asking each if he or she would answer just a single question if it was asked by one of her students. Who could refuse that? I have been writing replies to her students ever since, for example to Minami Funakoshi, whose question had to do with my book *The Pine Barrens* and a couple of people in a tarpaper shanty. Minami said, "You have many quotes in the story that capture Fred and Bill's voices and personalities as well. Some of my favourites are: 'Come in. Come in. Come on the hell in' and 'I didn't paper this year. . . . For the last couple months, I've had sinus.' I was curious—do you know right away when you hear a quote you want to include in the story, or do you usually mine for it through your notes?"

Dear Minami—Across my years as a writer and a writing teacher, I have been asked myriad questions about the reporting and compositional process but not before now this basic one of yours. And the answer comes forth without a moment's contemplation: I know right away when I hear a quote I'll want to include in the story. . . . In interviews, I scribble and scribble, gathering impressions, observations, information, and quotes, but not altogether mindlessly. Writing is selection. From the first word of the first sentence in an actual composition, the writer is choosing, selecting, and deciding (most importantly) what to leave out. In a broader, less efficient way, that is what goes on during the scribbling of interview notes. I jot down everything that strikes me as having any potentiality whatever to be useful in the future composition, and since I am learning on the job and don't know what the piece will be like, I scoop up, say, ten times as much stuff as I'll ultimately use. But when Fred Brown says "Come in. Come in. Come on the hell in," I come in, sit down, and soon jot the line. I don't have to be Nostradamus to sense that his form of greeting will be useful, any more than I could resist his remark about papering and his sinuses. Factual writing is also a kind of treasure hunt, and when the nuggets come along

you know what they are. They often provide beginnings
and endings, even titles. In interior Alaska, non-native
people often describe one another in terms of when
they "came into the country." That phrase is repeated so
much it is almost a litany, and I heard it so often that I
had a title for "Coming into the Country" long before
any of it was written. That was lucky and rare, because
titles are usually very hard to choose.

•

Among the three or four dozen pieces Woody Allen has con-
tributed to *The New Yorker*, the first one seemed to his editor,
Roger Angell, to contain an overabundance of funny lines. He
told Allen that even if the jokes were individually hilarious
they tended cumulatively to diminish the net effect. He said
he thought the humor would be improved if Allen were to leave
some of them out.

Sculptors address the deletion of material in their own
analogous way. Michelangelo: "The more the marble wastes,
the more the statue grows." Michelangelo: "Every block of stone
has a statue inside it, and it is the task of the sculptor to discover
it." Michelangelo, loosely, as we can imagine him with six tons
of Carrara marble, a mallet, a point chisel, a pitching tool, a
tooth chisel, a claw chisel, rasps, rifflers, and a bush hammer:
"I'm just taking away what doesn't belong there."

And inevitably we have come to Ernest Hemingway and
the tip of the iceberg—or, how to fashion critical theory from
one of the world's most venerable clichés. "If a writer of prose
knows enough about what he is writing about he may omit things
that he knows and the reader, if the writer is writing truly
enough, will have a feeling of those things as strongly as though
the writer had stated them. The dignity of movement of an
iceberg is due to only one-eighth of it being above water." The
two sentences are from *Death in the Afternoon,* a nonfiction

book (1932). They apply as readily to fiction. Hemingway sometimes called the concept the Theory of Omission. In 1958, in
an "Art of Fiction" interview for *The Paris Review*, he said to
George Plimpton, "Anything you know you can eliminate and
it only strengthens your iceberg." To illustrate, he said, "I've
seen the marlin mate and know about that. So I leave it out.
I've seen a school (or pod) of more than fifty sperm whales in
that same stretch of water and once harpooned one nearly
sixty feet in length and lost him. So I left that out. All the stories I know from the fishing village I leave out. But the knowledge is what makes the underwater part of the iceberg."

In other words:

> There are known knowns—there are things we know
> we know. We also know there are known unknowns.
> That is to say, we know there are some things we do not
> know. But there are also unknown unknowns—the ones
> we don't know we don't know.

Yes, the influence of Ernest Hemingway evidently extended
to the Pentagon.

Be that as it might not be, Ernest Hemingway's Theory of
Omission seems to me to be saying to writers, "Back off. Let
the reader do the creating." To cause a reader to see in her
mind's eye an entire autumnal landscape, for example, a writer
needs to deliver only a few words and images—such as corn
shocks, pheasants, and an early frost. The creative writer leaves
white space between chapters or segments of chapters. The
creative reader silently articulates the unwritten thought that
is present in the white space. Let the reader have the experience. Leave judgment in the eye of the beholder. When you
are deciding what to leave out, begin with the author. If you
see yourself prancing around between subject and reader, get

lost. Give elbow room to the creative reader. In other words, to the extent that this is all about you, leave that out.

"Creative nonfiction" is a term that is currently having its day. When I was in college, anyone who put those two words together would have been looked upon as a comedian or a fool. Today, Creative Nonfiction is the name of the college course I teach. Same college. Required to give the course a title, I named it for a quarterly edited and published by Lee Gutkind, then at the University of Pittsburgh. The title asks an obvious question: What is creative about nonfiction? It takes a whole semester to try to answer that, but here are a few points: The creativity lies in what you choose to write about, how you go about doing it, the arrangement through which you present things, the skill and the touch with which you describe people and succeed in developing them as characters, the rhythms of your prose, the integrity of the composition, the anatomy of the piece (does it get up and walk around on its own?), the extent to which you see and tell the story that exists in your material, and so forth. Creative nonfiction is not making something up but making the most of what you have.

•

When I worked at *Time*, after at last escaping Miscellany I wrote for five years in the back-of-the-book section called Show Business. In a typical week, the section consisted of three or four short pieces probably averaging nine hundred words. After you finished a piece, it entered the system in a pneumatic tube. When you next saw it, it bore the initials of your senior editor. It also had his [sic] revisions on it. You left your cubicle, paper in hand, went to the senior editor's office, and, in a mealy way, complained. Revisions might ensue. The piece then went to the managing editor, whose initials usually joined the senior editor's without ado, but not always. At last, with both sets of initials intact, the piece went to a department called Makeup, whose personnel could have worked as floral arrangers, because *Time*, in those days, unlike its rival *Newsweek*, never assigned a given length but waited for the finished story before fitting it into the magazine.

After four days of preparation and writing—after routinely staying up almost all night on the fourth night—and after tailoring your stories past the requests, demands, fine tips, and incomprehensible suggestions of the M.E. and your senior editor, you came in on Day 5 and were greeted by galleys from Makeup with notes on them that said "Green 5" or "Green 8" or "Green 15" or some such, telling you to condense the text by that number of lines or the piece would not fit in the magazine. You were supposed to use a green pencil so Makeup would know what could be put back, if it came to that. I can't remember it coming to that.

Groan as much as you liked, you had to green nearly all your pieces, and greening was a craft in itself—studying your completed and approved product, your "finished" piece, to see what could be left out. In fifty years, *The New Yorker*'s makeup department has asked me only once to remove some lines so a piece would fit. *The New Yorker* has the flexibility of spot drawings to include or leave out, and cartoons of varying and variable dimensions, and poems that can be there or not be there. Things fit, even if some things have to wait a week or two, or six months. Greening has stayed with me, though, because for four decades I have inflicted it on my college writing students, handing them nine or ten swatches of photocopied prose, each marked "Green 3" or "Green 4" or whatever.

Green 4 does not mean lop off four lines at the bottom, I tell them. The idea is to remove words in such a manner that no one would notice that anything has been removed. Easier with some writers than with others. It's as if you were removing freight cars here and there in order to shorten a train—or pruning bits and pieces of a plant for reasons of aesthetics or plant pathology, not to mention size. Do not do violence to the author's tone, manner, nature, style, thumbprint. Measure cumulatively the fragments you remove and see how many lines would be gone if the prose were reformatted. If you kill a widow, you pick up a whole line.

I give them thirty-two lines of Joseph Conrad "going up that river . . . like travelling back to the earliest beginnings of the world, when vegetation rioted on the earth and the big trees were kings." Green 3, if you dare. I give them Thomas McGuane's ode to the tarpon as grand piano (twenty lines, Green 3), Irving Stone's passionate declaration of his love of stone (nine lines, Green 1), Philip Roth's character Lonoff the novelist describing the metronomic boredom of the writing process in prose that metronomically repeats itself to make its point (try greening that), twenty-five lines, Green 3. I ask them to look up the first three pieces they have written for the course, to choose the one they preferred working on, then green ten per cent. And I give them the whole of the Gettysburg Address (twenty-five lines, Green 3). Memorization and familiarity have made that difficult, yes, but scarcely impossible. For example, if you green the latter part of sentence 9 and the first part of sentence 10, you can attach the head of 9 to the long tail of 10 and pick up twenty-four words, nine per cent of Abraham Lincoln's famously compact composition:

> 9. It is for us the living, rather, to be dedicated here
> 10. to the great task remaining before us . . .

At *Time*, Calvin Trillin was a colleague, as he has been throughout my years with *The New Yorker*. In a piece for *The New Yorker*'s Web site, he wrote about his own memories of greening and the lessons it imparted:

I don't have any interest in word games—I don't think I've ever done a crossword or played Scrabble—but I found greening a thoroughly enjoyable puzzle. I was surprised that what I had thought of as a tightly constructed seventy-line story—a story so tightly constructed that it had resisted the inclusion of that maddening leftover fact—was unharmed, or even improved, by greening ten per cent of it. The greening I did in Time Edit convinced me that just about any piece I write could be improved if, when it was supposedly ready to hand in, I looked in the mirror and said sternly to myself "Green fourteen" or "Green eight." And one of these days I'm going to begin doing that.

•

Aaron Shekey, an app designer out of Dane County, Wisconsin— a rock composer and bandleader, too—works in Minneapolis but is more than evidently nostalgic for the arresting silhouette of his boyhood city. Madison, the Wisconsin capital, stands on a morainal isthmus between two glacial lakes, which are not small. The hotels, office buildings, and apartment complexes of central Madison rise no more than a hundred and ninety feet, forming an accordant skyline. On his Web site, Shekey described it in a short essay called "It's What You Leave Out." Only the dome of the capitol of Wisconsin projects above all other structures. It's like El Greco's Toledo but without the exaggeration. It's as striking as Mont-Saint-Michel. How has that come to be? In 1915, while the building was under construction, the City of Madison decreed that no new structure could rise higher than the base of the dome and the Corinthian columns of the capitol's façade. No variance has ever been granted. The scene is spectacular across water. Shekey the musician closes with a quote from the script of the movie *Almost Famous*: "It's not what you put into it. It's what you leave out. . . . Yeah, that's rock 'n' roll."

Or, in the words of the literary critic Harold Bloom, writing on Shakespeare: "Increasingly in his work, what he leaves out becomes much more important than what he puts in, and so he takes literature beyond its limits."

•

When I was a sophomore in college, I went to Scarsdale, New York, a few days before Christmas to visit a roommate named Louis Marx. In the nineteen-twenties, his father—also named Louis Marx—and his uncle David Marx had founded Louis Marx and Company, maker of toys. Now, in 1950, it was, as Louis Sr. seemed to enjoy saying, "the biggest toy company in the world—bigger than Lionel and Gilbert put together." Having grown up making architectural structures from A. C. Gilbert Erector sets, and with Lionel O-gauge streamliners running all over my attic, I was much impressed. On various occasions in Scarsdale, I had also been much impressed by the sorts of people who dropped in at the Marx house—General Omar Bradley, for example, and General Curtis LeMay, and General Walter Bedell Smith. This was five years after the end of the Second World War, in which Omar Bradley, five stars, supervised the invasion of Germany, and Walter Bedell Smith, four stars, was the chief of staff, Supreme Headquarters Allied Expeditionary Force, and Curtis LeMay, four stars, organized the bombing of Japan. Marx toys were inventive windup machines—little tinplate tanks, cars, fire engines, boats, a fourteen-and-a-half-inch G-man pursuit car—logoed with a large "X" over the letters "M A R." Like his son, Louis Jr., Louis Sr. was a swift quipper, and I loved just listening to him talk. I had to be in New York City later on this particular day, and Louis Sr. offered me a ride, saying that he had an errand there, too. I said goodbye to my contemporaries (I had dated one of my roommate's sisters) and went down the driveway in a chauffeur-driven town car with their father and stepmother.

So this is the situation: Two-thirds of a century later, I am describing that ride to New York City in a piece on the writing process that is focused on the principle of leaving things out. I am with Mr. and Mrs. Monarch of Toys, whose friends a few years ago led various forms of the invasion of Europe. Do I leave that out? Help! Should I omit the lemony look on General Smith's face the day he showed up late for lunch after his stomach was pumped? I am writing this, not reading it, and I don't know what to retain and what to reject. The monarchical remark on being greater than the sum of Lionel and Gilbert— do I leave that out? I once saw Mr. Marx toss a broiled steak onto a rug so his bulldog could eat it. How relevant is that? Do I leave that out? Will it offend his survivors? In a recent year, his great-granddaughter was a sophomore in my college writing course. Her name was Barnett, not Marx. I did not know her beforehand, and had not even learned that my old roommate's grandniece was at Princeton, when her application for a place in the course came in. "You gave my grandmother her first kiss," it began. How relevant is that? Should I cut that out? Mrs. Marx—Idella, the stepmother of my roommate—was rumored among us Princeton sophomores of the time to be the sister of Lili St. Cyr. In the twenty-first century, in whose frame of reference is the strip dancer Lili St. Cyr? Better to exclude that? Best to exclude that Idella danced, too? This is about what you leave out, not what you take off. Writing is selection.

A glass partition separated the chauffeur from his passengers, soundproofing our conversation. Mr. Marx said the driver was new. Chauffeurs are good for about six months, he said. For two months, they are learning to work for you. Then for two months they are excellent. Then they start to steal from you, and two months later you fire them. Please! How much of this is germane? The car, meanwhile, has slid down the Hutchinson River Parkway and turned west on the Cross County Parkway and south on the Saw Mill and the Henry Hudson Parkway to the city. It exits at 125th Street and before long draws up at 60 Morningside Drive. Until this moment, I have had no idea where Mr. and Mrs. Marx are going. At 60 Morningside, Mr. Marx asks me if, before I continue on my way downtown (by subway), I would like to meet General Eisenhower.

This was President's House, Columbia University, and Eisenhower was the eponymous resident. Inside, under a high ceiling, was a large, lighted Christmas tree, the Eisenhower family milling around. Soon after we had all been introduced, Mr. Marx and General Eisenhower moved toward an elevator that would take them to the highest of six floors, where Ike had a studio in which he painted. The purpose of Mr. Marx's visit, it became clear, was for him to choose one of Ike's paintings, which Ike would give him as a gift. Merry Christmas. Mrs. Marx stayed downstairs with Mrs. Eisenhower. Mr. Marx and the General told me to come along with them. The three of us ascended to the studio— a spacious attic awash in natural light. Ike had lined up half a dozen finished pictures for Mr. Marx to consider. Near them, on an easel in the center of the room, was Ike's current project, an unfinished still-life. The subject was a square table covered with a red-checked tablecloth and a bowl of fruit—apples, plums, and pears, topped by a bunch of grapes. After studying for a time the paintings from which he was to choose, Mr. Marx said that he needed to pee. He would choose, eventually and shrewdly, a large canvas of the principal buildings of the United States Military Academy from across the parade ground. Meanwhile, Ike told him where he could find a bathroom on a lower floor. Mr. Marx went to the elevator and disappeared.

Now General Eisenhower and I were alone in his studio.

What on earth to say—with those five stars in pentimento on his shoulders, me a nineteen-year-old college student. The problem was more his than mine, but for him it was not a problem. He began to talk about the red-checked tablecloth and bowl of fruit. He said that when he was growing up in Abilene, Kansas, his world was symbolized by tablecloths just like this one, and that was why this current project meant so much to him. The still-life was well along—the apples, plums, and pears deftly drawn and highlighted. Pretty much tongue-tied until now, at last I had something to ask. Despite the painting's advanced stage, it did not include the grapes.

I said, "Why have you left out the grapes?"

Ike said, "Because they're too God-damned hard to paint."